Born to *fly*

Pat Stark

Covenant
Publishing
House

Born to Fly
by Pat Stark
Published by Covenant Publishing House
26 Lake Wire Drive
PO Box 524
Lakeland, Fl. 33802-0524
www.covenantpublishinghouse.com

Editing, design and layout by Celoria, Inc., www.celoriainc.com
Cover art and design by Katie McFarlane

Copyright ©2010 Pat Stark

All rights reserved. No part of this publication may be reproduced,
stored in a retrieval system, or transmitted in any form or by any
means, electronic, mechanical, photocopying, recording, or otherwise,
without the prior written permission of the publisher.

Printed in the United States of America

ISBN: 978-0-615-39246-2

Some names and details of the story have been changed, and any
similarity between the names and stories of individuals described in
this book to individuals known to readers is purely coincidental.

All Scriptures, unless otherwisde indicated, are taken from the Holy
Bible, New International Version, ©1973, 1978, 1984, by International
Bible Society.

Dedication & Acknowledgements

This book is dedicated first and foremost to God the Father who was willing to send His Son Jesus into this broken world to pay the price of freedom for captives like me. To Jesus who has always been there to walk with me through the process of my healing, even when I couldn't see the next step before me. To the Holy Spirit who has encouraged me all along the way by speaking to my heart as well as speaking through His Word, people, and circumstances.

I also dedicate this book to Bruce for your patience as I sat hour after hour at the computer with my back to you; to Ginny, Ron, Marleen, and Evelyn for your invaluable help with comments, corrections, and editing; to The Covenant Center family who helped me begin this overwhelming process, especially to Heather who put up with my many questions and coordinated it all; to Katie McFarlane for your loving gift of the beautiful book cover; to all of you who believed I had something to say and who encouraged me with your words, finances, and in numerous other ways. You know who you all are and your reward will be great in heaven. Thank you from the bottom of my heart! You are all such a blessing to me.

Thank you, Jesus, for trusting me with this assignment and then leading me all the way through to its completion. Please use it for Your glory and give it wings to fly wherever it might be needed.

Forward

If this book seems a bit overwhelming to you, I suggest you read the Introduction as well as the first two or three chapters and then invite God to show you which chapter you are to read next. He knows exactly where you are on your particular journey and the next step needed to get you where you need to go. I love the map at the Mall because it simply tells us, "YOU ARE HERE." We can't get where we're going unless we begin with where we are. Which chapter jumps out at you or seems to draw your interest? Begin there.

The "rules" can tell us we have to start at the beginning and work through to the end, but I challenge you to get out of the box and allow the Holy Spirit to lead you according to His blueprint for your reading. However, I do suggest you read the last two chapters as well when you feel ready.

CONTENTS

INTRODUCTION:
BORN TO FLY LIKE AN EAGLE

Freed to Become Who We Were
Created to Be - Heart Hunger

"He gives strength to the weary and increases the power
of the weak. Even youths grow tired and weary, and
young men stumble and fall; but those who hope in the
Lord will renew their strength. They will soar on wings
like eagles; they will run and not grow weary, they will
walk and not be faint." Isaiah 40:29-31
The Lord, "Who satisfies your desires with good things so
that your youth is renewed like the eagle's."
Psalm 103:5

Thinking back to my childhood, what stands out most clearly is the loneliness I experienced, always feeling on the outside looking in at a world that was far too big, overwhelming, and fearful. My parents' preoccupation with their own struggles, fears, and inadequacies added to the false belief that I had to find my own way in order to cope with the uncertainties of life. Because I was a small child, however, there was no way to do this. Compounding the situation was the pain of sexual abuse I experienced while still a very young child through someone I had trusted. Internally, I felt like I was bleeding, but no one recognized it. At five or six, I remember lying on my bed desperately crying out for God to help me, but had no idea how to find Him except in a non-personal, religious way that didn't begin to touch the pain. As a result of the lurking fear and turmoil inside, I became very angry and controlling, but because of the mask I wore, most people who didn't know me very well were unaware. In fact, many of them thought I was actually quite sweet. I realize now that the one goal in my life was to keep my world safe at any cost.

Thankfully, in my late twenties, my inability to make life work the way I needed caught up with me and waves of overwhelming fear finally led me to find grace and peace through surrendering my life to Jesus. I discovered it to be just like the line in the wonderful hymn "Amazing Grace" reveals, "Twas grace that taught my heart to fear, and grace my fears relieved." After that I grew spiritually by leaps and bounds, but since I still carried all the painful, buried emotions of the past within me, they sometimes leaked out in ways that hurt others. As desperately as I wanted to be free from my anger and control, I was bound and remained hopelessly trapped. In fact, I had a host of buried emotions such as rejection, abandonment and shame, but remained totally disconnected from them. The pain of past rejection caused me to build a wall around my heart, but that only created more loneliness because it locked others out of my life. My struggle finally drove me to cry out with everything in me for Jesus to set this prisoner free and that desperate cry became the beginning of my own healing journey. My prayer throughout the writing of this book was that God would use the keys of healing He had given to me to bring any needed healing and freedom to you as well.

Some time into my healing journey, God began to reveal a glimpse of the eagle hidden within me. I began to see I was born to fly, but because of the hurts experienced from living in a sin-filled world, I felt grounded with broken wings. Instead of flying like the eagle I was created to be, I was feeling more like a chicken scratching in the dirt even though somewhere deep inside was a deep longing to become who I really was.

During a difficult part of that season, as I would walk a three-mile path around one of the beautiful lakes in our town, there above the majestic steeple of the large church I would see an eagle perched on top of the cross. The eagle wasn't there all the time, but when it was, I was filled with the hope and joy that one day I would become like that eagle and soar the way God had always intended me to.

Free to Become Who We Were Originally Created to Be

God is a healer, a restorer, and a releaser of the captive. He came to open the prison doors and to set the captives free. Free to do what? Free to become who we were created to be and free to co-labor with Him in the particular garden He longs to place us in. There is more to life than existing; life is meant to be lived with Him and for Him, fulfilling the purposes He placed within our hearts even before we are ever born.

To see others set free to become who they are also created to be is the purpose for this book. It contains some of the things I have learned along my journey that can help you cooperate with Jesus so the pain from your past can be released and healing can come to your broken heart. As freedom comes, you can begin to hear more clearly His invitation to join Him in bringing freedom to other captives as well. Because Jesus is a redeemer and a restorer, all the enemy has stolen or subtracted from your personality, God means to give back in order that His purposes for you can be fulfilled. Even further, that healing can then begin to be multiplied out to countless others when you dare to join with Him for your own restoration.

In Isaiah 61:1 we discover a prophecy regarding the mission of Jesus in releasing us, the captives, to become who we were always meant to be. "The Spirit of the Sovereign Lord is upon me, because the Lord has anointed me to preach good news to the poor. He has sent me to bind up the brokenhearted, to proclaim freedom for the captives, and release from darkness for the prisoners."

"In a desert land he found him, in a barren and howling waste. He shielded him and cared for him; he guarded him as the apple of his eye, like an eagle that stirs up its nest and hovers over its young, that spreads its wings to catch them and carries them on its pinions." (Deuteronomy 32:10-13)

Our Journey Begins with Hunger

We were created with hunger, just look at any newborn. It's easy to forget that our hunger isn't for physical satisfaction alone, even though we often live like it is because of the hurts we've experienced that have closed down our hearts. The failure to thrive in some newborns because of severe emotional neglect reminds us, however, that more than physical food is needed. Even though we might not have experienced anything near that kind of neglect, the emotional need that has been put within us still gets thwarted and disappointed many times over, sometimes even by those who have loved us. As a result, little by little we learn to hide our true selves and deaden our hearts from deep desires.

"Come, all you who are thirsty, come to the waters; and you who have no money, come, buy and eat! Come, buy wine and milk without money and without cost. Why spend money on what is not bread, and your labor on what does not satisfy? Listen, listen to me, and eat what is good, and your soul will delight in the richest of fare." (Isaiah 55:1,2)

Why are we not hungrier for God? Why do we so easily get distracted and seemingly become satisfied with so many lesser things, burying our hunger under the busyness of life and the mundane demands of everyday survival? If we're honest, sometimes the appeal to hunger spiritually just makes us feel guilty, like there's one more thing to do and we're falling short. Could it be that we have not been able to come to the source from which all true life flows because our hearts have been covered over even without our awareness?

"For with you is the fountain of life; in your light we see light." (Psalm 36:9)

Living in a broken world has taken its toll on all of us just through the hurts we've experienced throughout our lives, some that were minor and some that were deep. As the wounds have collected through the years, never being fully healed, they often caused us to protect and cover our hearts. Before long we either no longer feel very hungry or we are starved and seek satisfaction from something else. Sometimes women turn to relationships to satisfy and men may strive for success. I see this too often in needy women (and some men) who have tried to gain their identity from their relationships and who cannot seem to survive without someone to give them worth. Of course that's an illusion because our value cannot come from people or our work, but only from God Himself, so it usually doesn't work very well for long.

I know some who have lost themselves in their work, becoming workaholics and avoiding relationships on any deep level because the workplace feels safer and more manageable. There are many other things we use to deaden ourselves as well, things like food, alcohol, drugs, shopping, sex or sports. We might even use TV, books, movies, the Internet or video games to create a painless, fantasy world for ourselves, one in which we can become an observer instead of taking risk. We might have focused most of our attention on those parts of us that were accepted, like our intellect, our spirit or our body, while neglecting the rest. For many years I hid myself in the spiritual because that came easily to me and was applauded, especially in the church.

Our hunger is in the heart, but since it no longer feels safe to live connected to our vulnerable heart, it's easier to cover it over and attempt to satisfy ourselves on a lesser level. "Keep your heart with all diligence, for out of it spring the issues of life" (Proverbs 4:23 NKJV). Instead of keeping or watching over our heart, we have often neglected and abandoned it, even without realizing it. Very gradually, our hearts become increasingly hidden and we begin to lose the real self that is in the deepest part of our being, deadening our true passions.

Unfortunately, even though we've ignored them, our desires are still there and will often come out in uncontrollable twisted ways like anger, fear or lust. In order to remain protected and still find substitute worth, we sometimes become more like human doings rather than human beings. One young man I helped on his healing journey was always ready to serve with his hands, giving of himself continually, yet remaining totally disconnected on the heart level. He gave his hands to people, but not his heart. As that young man did, we can also *do things* to get our identity and try to find our worth in various ways, sometimes using things like work, relationships or maybe even ministry. Now those are all good God-given things meant to bring joy and satisfaction, but when they are used to attempt to fill our hungry hearts, they become corrupted.

Who are we deep within our hearts and how do we get the true satisfaction we're starved for? Becoming who we were originally created to be is a process, a journey of the heart. Since the majority of us have gotten hurt along the journey, what have we done with our pain? Not knowing what else to do, we buried the pain, tried to kill our longings, and attempted to move on without realizing that those hidden emotions have become obstacles to living our lives to the fullest. A number of years ago, God called to me through Isaiah 57:14 and said, "Build up, build up, prepare the road! Remove the obstacles out of the way of my people." He knew that His people were starving because for many of us, our hunger, longings, and desires had been buried a long time ago. Sometimes those buried longings and desires surface as demands that others come through for us, that life work for us in the way we need it to or even that life in this broken world be fair. We develop a spirit of entitlement. Then when none of those things happen, we can become angry, blame others or become depressed.

One of the reasons we often deny our pain and hide ourselves from our buried passions is because we seem to have survived intact and, at least on the surface of our lives, we look pretty good. If we are healthy emotionally, then why, if we are to be really honest with ourselves, are we not feeling free or experiencing deep, lasting satisfaction on more than a superficial level? To make matters worse, why do those buried emotions sometimes leak out causing problems in our lives and relationships? When triggered, we might find ourselves struggling with annoying emotions like resentment, fear, anxiety, jealousy or perhaps even anger, disappointment, powerlessness, guilt or sadness. Where are those feelings coming from? How many times have we been around someone with buried anger who feels like they're a volcano ready to erupt, causing us to walk on egg shells?

We might be people who feel numb or dead inside, or perhaps struggle with emotions that lurk just beneath the surface, waiting to erupt given the right circumstance. Why are we so good at avoiding our feelings when things begin to become overwhelming or uncomfortable? When life seems to slow a bit, when nothing is distracting us, we might even begin to feel like something is missing, that there has to be more, but too many times we don't know what it is or how to find it.

Our unhealed, buried emotions affect us in so many different ways. We might over-react to real or perceived rejection and feel isolated, forgotten, lonely, and alone, or we might fear failure and struggle often with our self-worth. One woman who came for healing misinterpreted everything I said, twisting it to make it into a rejection of her, which of course was not the way it was meant. It is common for people with unhealed emotions to read into another's words or actions things that are not true. Because of unhealed hurt, they view life through their own painful rejection, so they are unable to give others even the right to have a bad day!

Though our struggles have caused many of us to become brokenhearted without even realizing it, these wounds do not have to continue to define, thwart, and rule our lives. To rediscover ourselves in the depths of our being is a process, but it's a part of the journey that the Father, Son and Spirit want to help us with. As we learn how to cooperate and co-labor with Jesus in that process, it's amazing to experience the changes that begin to happen.

God is doing major healing in the area of broken hearts and wounded emotions these days, but He needs our cooperation. This is all part of the process of becoming who we were created to be, however, it requires our willingness to co-labor with His Spirit and our honest openness to face what we might have been trying to run and hide from for many years. We might even be those who are admired and looked up to by others and, although it feels good for the moment, a dull emptiness remains along with the lingering desire to be truly known and accepted. Admiration is nice, but it's like a figurine on a shelf that you might enjoy viewing, yet never love or connect with on a deep level of the heart. I desired to be admired for many years because, as I see now, I was afraid to be known enough to be really loved.

Over the course of my healing journey that has spanned more than thirty years, I've learned some things about myself. The first was to recognize the fear I had of trusting God, stemming from unhealed betrayal in early childhood. Since healing requires us to trust God, my process was definitely slowed. Another was that I was stubborn and not always willing to let go of whatever I falsely believed necessary for my survival. Third, I resisted change because I disliked having to face the emotions I buried in order to keep from feeling in the first place. Through it all, though, I learned that finally becoming free to be who I was created to be was well worth facing any pain necessary for healing. As I became more whole within, there was an increase of integrity, peace, and joy. I also experienced new expressions of creativity as well a general sense of well-being. I am finding that it's becoming increasingly fun to be me! Although this process continues in some form all of our lives, the difficult part of it does not have to take others as long as it has taken me. As I'm involved in helping people these days, I'm witnessing a wonderful grace from God to speed up the process for those who will join with Him on this journey of healing.

Through this book, my desire is to help shorten your process and to help you to co-labor with Jesus in the healing He has provided for you. When we are willing to cooperate with God's Spirit for our own healing, we can become *wounded healers* to others, sometimes without our even being aware of it. For example, when parents are willing to enter the process for themselves, their children get the overflow. They begin to parent in a healthier manner, enabling them not to overreact or to distance themselves from their children's painful emotions, but instead to walk with them through the hurtful times in a more connected, healthy way. I recently observed this in a member of my family who was able to walk with her young son through a fearfully, disappointing time in his life with increased empathy, compassion, and strength.

From the beginning of my own journey, God has used me to walk with others to help them heal from damage done simply through living in a broken world with other wounded, imperfect people. Wounded people wound others. As I look back over my own life, I see how I have also unintentionally wounded others many times over including my own family. To give you an example, my own unhealed rejection caused me to try to over-protect my children when they were young. I held them back from experiencing some of the normal activities of childhood because of my fear they would be hurt or rejected, instead of just help-ing them through any hurt that came their way. As a result of not facing my own unhealed fear at that time, I sadly passed my spirit of fear on to them.

Looking back to the beginning of my healing journey, I see how little I knew but even so, God began to use me to help others find their freedom in the way I had longed for someone to help me. Although wounded people wound others, people who are in the process of being healed can be used by God to help bring healing to those around them. I want to be clear that it is God who is the healer, so we begin by praying for our healing, however it's not usually until we join forces with Him, co-laboring for our own emotional restoration, that we see lasting change happen.

Would you be willing to ask Jesus to search out any unhealed places in you that might be sabotaging your life and relationships and keeping you from all you were created to be? Would you then join me on a journey of cooperation with God in healing and restor-ing any hurtful places that might still be lodging in your soul?

Scripture

"Come to me, all you who are weary and burdened, and I will give you rest." Matthew 11:28

1
BIGGER PICTURE OF LIFE

Finding Your True Self,
Moving Toward Freedom

---

*"My frame was not hidden from you when I was made in
the secret place, when I was woven together in the depths
of the earth, your eyes saw my unformed body. All the
days ordained for me were written in your book before
one of them came to be." Psalm 139:15,16*
*"For he chose us in him before the creation of the
world..." Ephesians 1:4*

You have been invited to be *you*. The *you* that perhaps you have only gotten glimpses of, the *you* that got lost under the pain and disappointments of life. The *you* that is locked up inside in a dark place, crying out for *food* that really satisfies. The *you* that has been lost behind a closed door and forgotten. The *you* that can experience joy and peace in the midst of an unfair and broken world.

Before you were ever born, you were known, seen, and valued (Ephesians 1:4-6; Psalm 139:1,13-16). You were wanted and desired and your life was not an accident no matter what circumstances surrounded your birth. Despite your feelings to the contrary, you are not illegitimate or orphaned and you are invited to be a part of a perfect family, a family where true love flows between the members and where there is joy, acceptance, value, and honor. That perfect family is the Trinity; Father, Son, and

Holy Spirit. They are the only perfect family and are inviting you to join them. There is a seat at their table - a place card with your name on it! No one else can sit there and, if you do not come, that seat will remain empty. It's your seat; no one can take it away from you or replace you in it. That can seem too good to be true, because for most of us, we have felt replaced or overlooked many times over, if not outright rejected and betrayed. Sometimes that even happens in our own families.

Somewhere deep within, we have all longed for that perfect family where we will be seen, accepted, enjoyed, truly known, and valued. However, on this earth we are often disappointed in that longing. We find it easier to give up and just bury our longings, but in order for that to happen, we must kill parts of our heart. Hidden deep inside we still have the desire to be enjoyed, accepted, and included, yet at the same time we can secretly fear being tossed aside in a relationship or a job.

Without my realizing it at the time, because of the loneliness of my childhood, I developed a people addiction. An addiction like that can cause us to feel driven to please everyone and to use friends in order to not be alone. To keep from being thrown away, I over-worked relationships for years without ever realizing that wasn't normal. For example, I took care of everyone, trying to keep them happy with me so I wouldn't be abandoned. Too many times I gave more importance to the needs of those on the outside than I did to my own family's needs. Looking back on those days now causes grief in my heart, but sadly I cannot make up for what the enemy has stolen, only God can do that.

When we have experienced a number of disappointed desires, we can begin to forget our longings and live from outside of our hearts. We try to please others, offer our services, produce much, and perform well in order to be approved of, but the deepest part of us is buried and lost. Through the years I've met so many I would love to have really known, but it was impossible because their heart was covered over years before. They were often talented, efficient, pleasant, and helpful, but not more than a superficial connection could be made since their hearts were buried because of the hurtful circumstances that caused them to be wounded.

We get glimpses of life the way it was originally meant to be when we experience that perfect moment and all seems good, but then it quickly vanishes into an argument, a disappointment or loss. Once again, we are left empty. It's often like a picnic on a perfect day with the temperature just right, glorious blue sky overhead, and fun people to be with. It's just then that the annoying flies come and seem to ruin everything. We are so busy swatting flies that we lose sight of all we were enjoying before. We allow ourselves to be robbed.

The reality is that we were created for the Garden. The Garden of Eden where everything was perfect and God's wonderful creation was unspoiled. Adam and Eve were free to passionately enjoy all that God created except for the tree of the knowledge of good and evil in the middle. There were no tears, no disappointments or sorrow and no flies to spoil the picnic. They were free to live happily ever after. Sadly though, after being lured by the enemy to doubt God's good, giving heart, Adam and Eve chose the enemy's lure to be their own god and do things their own way. That is a temptation we all struggle with to this very day. When God doesn't come through for us in the way we believe we desperately need, it becomes easy to doubt His goodness and try to find a way to handle things ourselves. Out of concern that they would eat from the tree of Life and live in that fallen, hopeless state forever, God had to put Adam and Eve out of the Garden.

Our longings, just like theirs, are still for the perfection of the Garden; we still *long* to "live happily ever after," the way we were always meant to live. We believe that we can still attain it in this broken world if we just try hard enough or find the right person, place or things to satisfy us. Those longings, when unmet, often turn into demands and feelings of entitlement. This can cause us to strive harder to prove we are acceptable through what we acquire or, even without realizing it, we may silently demand others accept us to give us our worth so we can feel happy. What we are really demanding is the Garden, a world that is perfect. Looking at it on a day-to-day superficial level, why else do we get so angry when a driver cuts us off, someone steps in front of us in a grocery line or our plans go awry? On a much more serious note, how often do we get angry when we feel betrayed by someone we trusted? The truth is we don't want to live in a broken world because it hurts too much and feels far too uncertain.

Obviously, God's children no longer live in the Garden, but facing the reality of living in a fallen world can be very fearful and difficult. Choosing to deny seeing things the way they are seems so preferable! In facing the uncertainty of life the way it really is, there are many scary, painful circumstances with feelings attached to them that we will have to examine. Fear of death, divorce, messed-up children, illness, loss of friendship, financial difficulties, and job loss are just a few of the circumstances that cause us fear and pain. That's why coming to a new level of trust in the only One who holds all things together becomes essential if we are ever to rest. The problem is God doesn't always do things the way we want Him to and this makes us wonder if He is really good. If we are to trust Him, we have to wrestle with this whole area of *goodness*. Is God's heart still *good* when He doesn't do things as I desire or believe I need them done? Could I be misunderstanding *goodness* and does my definition have to change? Could the following scripture actually be true? "And we know that all that happens to us is working for our good if we love God and are fitting into His plans" (Romans 8:28 LNT).

We can have another problem with trusting as well. Experiencing betrayal of any kind destroys trust, so when we have been wounded through some very painful circumstance in our lives, it seems almost impossible to trust God deeply. The good news is that if we will honestly begin to face these things, we can come to a new place of desperate dependency upon God and along with it, a new passionate love, peace, security, and rest in Him. Now realize that we will have to face the truth that we don't really know how *to do life* and that we were never meant to do it alone. That independent spirit we inherited came in through the fall of man, but in reality, we were created to be dependent on the only One who is true life. We will have to face our real hunger and the truth that we can't fill it ourselves. This will create desperation for His life to be lived in and through us! Jesus says, *"I am the way* (through life), *the truth* (about life), *and the life"* (the only life worth living) (John 14:6). We often see that scripture only in reference to eternal life and it is, but eternal life begins now!

"Come to me, all you who are weary and burdened, and I will give you rest. Take my yoke upon you and learn from me, for I am gentle and humble in heart, and you will find rest for your souls. For my yoke is easy and my burden is light." (Matthew 11:28-30)

Don't you prefer to be yoked with Him since He knows how to do life and is the only way to get us there? I do! For so many years, I tried to hold my world together and attempted to control my life and the lives around me in order to feel secure. Because of feeling so unsafe from childhood, I needed to control all aspects of my world or, deep inside, I believed it would fall apart. I couldn't trust God with that job because others I put my trust in had betrayed me and this convinced me that God wasn't safe either. Oh, I loved God and served Him, but I didn't trust Him, not truly in the deepest part of my heart. Deep down, God wasn't safe because He might not do things the way I *needed* them to be done and then I would feel out of control! Even the thought was terrifying because it caused me to feel so helpless, just as I had as a child.

Many of us can live a life that is an illusion of the way our life was meant to be and then, because our pretense never works for long, we get disillusioned, angry, depressed or maybe even despairing. We can be silently angry at God because He is not cooperating with our plans although we are not usually even aware of our anger. You can sense the anger is there by the loss of desire to spend time with Him, feeling driven instead to the attraction of other things and the lure of temptation. For many of my days prior to healing, there would be times when God would feel distant. At that time, I'd notice the preference to read almost anything, even a cereal box, rather than the Bible! Why? Not realizing it, the reason was because I was unhappy when He wouldn't do things as I desired. Unconsciously, I was pulling away from Him, but it always felt more like He was leaving me. God doesn't leave, we do! Being disappointed with God may drive others to work harder, perform better or to find satisfaction in other things or relationships, but they never seem to bring any real lasting satisfaction.

Too often we take our displaced anger out on those around us, demanding they come through for us in ways they can't and because of that, we drive them away, at least emotionally. One woman I know put impossible demands on her husband to prove his love for her. There was no way he could jump through the right hoop and convince her, because her fear had come in years earlier and didn't originate with him. In frustration, he eventually gave up trying, began resenting her, and distanced himself even further through his work. Anger about our unmet needs can move into depression with a loss of energy and desire or it can get buried as unacknowledged resentment eventually turning into bitterness. Sometimes it drives us to try to *fix* our life and the lives of those around us, which we really can't, at least not for long. In any case, our joy for God and for living is robbed.

Fantasy and escape through movies, the Internet, books or maybe even daydreams become real temptations; a sterile life without the ache. We can look through the window at life without having to take any personal risks. We are often artists who paint pictures of our world the way we want it to be and then try to make it happen. We might even have a fantasy of the house with the white picket fence and the perfect family.

Sometimes we don't know where our pictures come from. One friend got her picture from a coffee advertisement in a magazine. The ad portrayed a loving couple sitting on the front porch with the dog at their feet. It was a warm, perfect picture that portrayed what she longed to create in her home, but the picture was an illusion.

I lived for many years as a Christian with low-grade depression resulting from my buried anger and resentment. Oh, I loved the Lord, but when He wouldn't cooperate with my plans, I held Him at arms length. I never turned my back on Him, for He was all I had, but without realizing it, I had walled off my heart years before I ever came to know Jesus. I had learned from the circumstances of life never to depend on or trust anyone, at least not on the deepest level of my heart.

Who is it that is feeding our emotions and deepening our despair? We often blame God, but in reality it is "the thief who comes to steal, kill and destroy" (John 10:10). Satan, the enemy who hates us, was the one who came to destroy the true life we were created to live. In their book, *The Sacred Romance*, Brent Curtis and John Eldredge, in referring to the enemy share, "The one purpose of his heart is the destruction of all that God loves, particularly His beloved." When we begin to realize this, it becomes apparent that we are in a war for our very lives, or at least for the life that is really life. They further state, "God and Satan each have a design, a battle plan, to capture our heart's devotion." Our hearts, as Jesus reminds us, cannot serve two masters (Matthew 6:24).

Moving Toward Freedom

Life in Jesus is meant to be a life of freedom and passion with true meaning and purpose.Honest reflection reveals that, for the most part, we're not there yet. Becoming who we are created to be requires a refining process that is not always comfortable. God will often allow what feels like destruction in our circumstances, but it is a destruction carefully designed to bring down only the systems we have created that hinder the fullness of the life we really hunger for. For example, we might have been carefully orchestrating our lives by trying to control our circumstances and the people around us because of past hurts without even realizing it. In God's merciful love, He allows our safe little world to begin to shake. Because we fear destruction, anger and anxiety surfaces and we blame God, circumstances, others or even ourselves. Coming to a new understanding of God's good heart toward us can help us see our hard circumstances from a different perspective. Joseph was able to see that larger picture and it was reflected in how he spoke to his brothers after they had acted in a cruel way against him. "But as for you, you meant evil against me, but God meant it for good" (Genesis 50:20). "And we know that in all things God works for the good of those who love Him, who have been called according to His purpose" (Romans 8:28 NKJV). We are also reminded that, "My thoughts are not your thoughts, neither are your ways, my ways, declares the Lord" (Isaiah 55:8). Coming to accept that His ways of accomplishment are far different than ours can help us to release the control we think we need and begin to trust His good heart toward us in new ways.

This is not the life God had originally created for us to live. It was not meant to look like this at all. Because of the lure of the enemy and the choices Adam and Eve made to be their own god and do things their own way, the life of the Garden was lost. However, we still have the longings buried deep within us for that perfect place. Jesus knows that and I believe He weeps as He repeatedly calls to us and waits. He waits for us to hear His voice and to join Him in the fight for the lives we were intended to live; to fight with Him, not against Him and to fight for and not against ourselves. Jesus longs for us to fight with Him for the restoration of the days that were "ordained for us" before the robbery from a broken world happened (Psalm 139:16).

What do those days look like? Do you even know? Many people don't, they never give it a thought. Instead they settle for day-to-day existence and too often those questions just get buried beneath religious duty. Because we don't feel called to minister in the church, the enemy whispers that we don't have a significant purpose with the exception of providing for our families, being nice moral people, and handling the mundane aspects of life the best we can. We miss the fact that our lives are needed and there is a significant piece that only we can bring.

Too often our days are misinterpreted and seen simply as

acquiring shallow external prosperity and success, but I believe there is an internal restoring God desires to do in our hearts so we are able to work with Him, not against Him, in the true purposes of our lives, co-laboring to bring forth His Kingdom on earth as it is in heaven.

Life is hard. You are in a war and you need to cooperate with Jesus for the life He sacrificed to give you. There is no question that eternal life is a free gift, but in order to become all that we are intended to be on this earth, we must enter the battle with Him for our very lives. You have a part to play at present. You were created on purpose for purpose and the enemy has been trying to steal those days God ordained for you, the days God saw before you were ever born.

Deep within our hearts are the purposes for which we are created, but they often get buried under years of debris so we don't even know what brings us life. We just get trapped in the duty of survival. In my early Christian life, it was often wrongly suggested that God would require of us the things we hate to do and send us where we never wanted to go. For me that was Africa. My fears had not yet been dealt with so the very thought of being sent to Africa evoked terror in my soul and made me want to run from God instead of to Him in trust. The enemy used lies like that to close my true heart even more and to develop an unhealthy fear of God. We need to get angry at the deceiver and the lies he uses to cripple us. God "hates robbery" and we should, too (Isaiah 61:8). We are often angry, but at the wrong things. We are not angry enough at the robbery, or at the thief who was a liar from the beginning.

Maybe the treasures within you were never seen, so they have never even been developed, but they are there just the same. It takes our willingness, however, to join with Jesus in mining for the treasure within. So many of us think there is no treasure there at all, only junk. I was one of those. I was never encouraged or believed in by anyone so although I saw treasure in others, I never saw it in myself. It has taken much time and courage to go there, but at just over 70 years old, I am finding things within myself I never knew existed. It is an exciting journey to discover ourselves - the true self that God has always known - and then begin to get a glimpse of the purposes for which we were created so we can begin to cooperate with Him in the process of getting us there.

Remember, it is the Spirit who searches out the deep things of our hearts. So will you invite Him to search within you to reveal the lies that were believed as truth, to restore the places within that were harmed through circumstances and through wounded, hurtful people? This is not about blaming, it is about facing the reality of exactly where we were wounded so we can begin to be healed in order to release forgiveness from our hearts. When we are willing to face the pain we have experienced in this broken world, we can begin to allow His healing process to restore us and bring forth the life God means for us to live.

Mining for the treasure often takes us through the pain of our past because the pain is often like the rock and debris that have been thrown in the stream of our lives. Picture in your mind a stream with huge boulders and trash dumped in it. If enough junk is thrown in that stream, the water no longer flows freely and it becomes polluted. The flow gets stopped up and we lose the vision of what the stream was originally meant to be, no longer enjoying the beauty or refreshing quality of the water, we see just the pollution and turn away in disgust. We settle for less than who we could be because it can be easier that way. Unfortunately, in our lives the rocks and debris have emotions wrapped around them, often painful emotions.

Those emotions were buried long ago because there was no one there to help us heal from them. We have felt abandoned and alone in those painful feelings, so we did the only thing we could do, stuffed them down deep inside and locked the door on them. Unfortunately, those emotions never really go away and, given the right triggers in the present, they leak out in hurtful ways that sabotage our lives and wound others. They can cause us to close the deepest parts of our heart toward God and other people even though we might be longing for relationship. It is my desire that through this book you will learn how to process and release those hurtful emotions because wounded people also wound others. Healed people can co-labor with God to become wounded healers.

Assignment

What do you love? Make a list of 5 or more things that you really love or enjoy then answer the following questions:
- Is there anything you currently do that exhilarates you and brings you life and joy? If so, what is it?
- If you could do anything at all without being held back, what would you do?

Are you willing to begin the journey with this prayer from Psalm 139:23-24 and then cooperate with God's Spirit in what He shows you? "Search me O God, and know my heart; test me and know my anxious thoughts. See if there is any hurtful way in me and lead me in the way everlasting."

God is a healing, restoring God, but healing takes place in the light. When things are buried within, they are kept in darkness and are left in a place where the enemy can bring torment.

After praying that prayer, continue to be patient. You might not see anything immediately, but keep your heart open. God knows the time when you are ready for Him to reveal these things to you.

In the beginning of my journey, I waited nine months for Him to reveal my very painful buried emotion of rejection. I realize with hindsight that I wasn't ready to face it when I first asked, even though I thought I was. Father knows best.

2
HIDDEN CHILD WITHIN

Set-ups and Triggers, Connecting Present and Past, Displacing Our Emotions, The Fullness of the Cross, Re-Nurturing

"But Jesus called the children to him and said, 'Let the little children come to me, and do not hinder them, for the kingdom of God belongs to such as these." Luke 18:16

In childhood, when we have been wounded through growing up in a negative emotional environment, or if we experienced a trauma of some kind, we can become stuck in some of our emotions. That can happen especially when there was no one to help us work through the feelings that resulted. The trauma could have been caused by abuse of any kind as well as any other type of deep hurt. It is common for us to tend to minimize abuse and deny the reality of any damage it might have caused. The abuse could have come through anyone and might have been verbal, emotional, physical or sexual. It could have come from a lack of parental nurture, love, protection, and care. Our wounding might have come out of a negative environment within the family, the neighborhood, the school or even the church. In that case, we might have gotten stuck in the particular emotion we felt at the moment or era in which it happened. Even though we continued to grow up overall, we remained emotionally imprisoned in the area of those old feelings. The fewer places in which we continue to be emotionally stuck, the better we are able to function in our adult lives.

When our hurt has been buried and the wound remains unhealed, the effect is similar to having an infection under our skin. The skin might scab over and it might appear that there has been healing, but any time there is a jarring, the wound reopens and the infection becomes apparent. Recently, after having some minor surgery for skin cancer, I was told not to allow the wound to scab over because they wanted it to heal from the inside out. The same principle applies with our emotions; we must first be healed on the inside. Otherwise, if the feeling gets triggered or jarred through a person or circumstance in the present, it can cause us to respond in a way that is out of proportion to the current situation. In other words, the infection leaks out.

A Set-up or Trigger

When we agree to co-labor with the Master Surgeon to bring healing to our hurts within, He will often use what I call a *set-up*. A set-up is simply a situation that triggers an emotional over-reaction to a present-day circumstance revealing that something deeper is going on. For example, you might find yourself reacting with anger or fear or in some way that is out of proportion to the current situation. Without your being able to control it, it's as if you are transported back to the age of the original trauma in which you experienced that particular emotion. In that case, you might be reacting out of a similar feeling that occurred in childhood or in your teens. If you were humiliated at age 13 by a teacher, your peers or someone of significance and a present situation occurs in which you fear being humiliated, you could experience an over-reaction of fear or shame. An emotional overreaction could also come from an unhealed adult experience such as the breakup of a marriage or a betrayal of some kind. It is important to keep in mind that the circumstance will not be exactly the same as in the past, but the emotion triggered will be similar.

When we over-react, our voices might rise, we might get defensively angry or want to hide and, whether we display the emotion or not, there is something going on inside even when we're not consciously aware of it. We might respond in a way that is more emotional than rational and usually our reaction is far out of proportion to the current situation. Let me give you an example of how the emotion of powerlessness can reveal itself. If we experienced feeling helpless or powerless as a child, perhaps due to a parent who wasn't there for us or maybe because of living with the uncertainty surrounding an alcoholic parent, we might be transported back to the helplessness of that child whenever we feel powerless in the present. So when a situation arises, such as a financial or relational crisis, we can tend to feel the same helplessness we experienced as a child. Our immediate outward reaction is often anger or fear, but we want to discover what feeling is being triggered beneath the anger and what pain from the past needs the healing touch of Jesus.

Through the years, I've found myself in emotionally-charged discussions with my husband when, instead of reacting like an adult, I began to sound like a young child or a rebellious teen who wants to act out when feeling pressured or controlled. I remember times when my husband and I sounded like two four-year-olds each competing to come out on top! My guess is that I'm not the only one who has ever reacted like that. In that moment, how old are we sounding? What feelings are being provoked within us as a result of the discussion?

If you suspect you might be experiencing such a set-up, ask yourself:

- "What am I feeling right now?" Name the emotion.
- "When did I feel this way before?" It might go all the way back to childhood.
- "God, please show me where this comes from so I can be healed from the past situation as well as the present one."

Again, if God allows an old memory to surface, pay attention to the feelings you felt in the original circumstance. Ask God to show you what those feelings were. How old were you? If it goes all the way back to age 9, it is the 9 year-old stuck within that needs the healing. Jesus is outside of time and exists in the past as well as the future.

When we allow the Holy Spirit to use those set-ups, asking Him to show us where the overreaction came from, sometimes a memory of some kind will come to mind, maybe even from early childhood. The memory might have nothing to do with the current situation and might not seem the same in any way, but the feeling we felt in both cases is similar. In identifying the emotion, we often discover we have an unhealed wound from the past that Jesus wants to heal. Allow the Spirit to show you that little child within you who carries your pain and begin to identify with him or her. *You* were that child and that was *your* pain - begin to own it. Without realizing it, for much of our lives *we* might have rejected and abandoned that little child within who carries our pain. Too often we have stuffed the child and the pain in a closet deep within and locked the door, but whenever it's triggered, the buried emotion leaks out to create new problems for us.

Let me give you an example from my own life. This might seem like a minor circumstance, but God has healed me in the same manner through many major painful situations as well. Whenever I got a phone call from a salesperson or telemarketer, I would overreact with anger and be horribly rude even though I didn't want to be. I felt trapped. In asking God to reveal where this was coming from, He showed me that as a child I often felt overpowered by the words of someone in my family. I felt pushed into a corner and trapped by their words as they talked *over* me and used me to talk *at*, but never allowed me to speak. As I connected the *memory with the emotion*, a healing took place that freed me to forgive the person who had their used words to overpower me. Almost immediately, I was freed to be able to have kind but firm boundaries with others who would try to overpower me with words, as well as with those salespeople and telemarketers who try to intrude.

It is natural for us to desire that others as well as ourselves act in an appropriate adult manner, however, when there are things that have not yet been healed from our past, the responses in those wounded areas are typically not logical or rational. Have you ever gotten annoyed at someone because their behavior was so childish or irresponsible? I know I have. In fact, I've become exasperated because it seems to me in that moment they're not an adult, but a child. What about those who continually repeat bad behaviors, but never seem to be able to learn anything from it? Some people have large portions of their life stuck in irresponsibility because of unhealed trauma from the past. That is not an excuse for bad behavior, because if we don't allow God's healing to come, we will continue to wound others around us, especially the ones we love. In fact, it's usually the ones we love so very much, who are harmed the most by our staying trapped by our old wounds.

When a traumatic situation happens to a child, they rarely have someone of wisdom to help them recognize the feelings that accompany it, so they do the only thing they are able - they bury those particular emotions or at least disconnect from them. The child distances itself from the pain even though they might retain the memory of the hurtful situation. The memory might even be able to be talked about freely, but without any emotion. I did that for years with a very traumatic, abusive situation that happened to me in my early teenage years. It was easy to talk about, in fact I even made it into a humorous story, but obviously there was a total disconnect from the pain because in reality it was devastating, certainly not funny. When I finally faced the pain of my emotions, I saw that the truth was that I had been traumatized and terrified! I was at home while my parents were on vacation when I experienced the horror of seeing a peeping Tom outside my bedroom window. I felt overcome with fear and helplessness, not knowing how to get any help because I felt trapped alone in my bedroom without a phone. How I coped afterward by making it into a humorous story was certainly a case of a separation between my head and my heart. The denial of the pain in my heart kept me imprisoned for years. My denial was finally broken at a seminar I attended where I realized for the first time that what I experienced was abuse.

Since no help was received earlier, the painful emotions remained lodged deep within. In order to survive the extreme helplessness that I felt, the pain had to be kept at a distance. Healing cannot come until both the head and heart connect to the pain.

The Present can be Connected to the Past

In the present, when the emotion is triggered and the pain surfaces, we rarely connect it with the circumstance that originally wounded us in the first place. Instead, our first response is to get angry and blame whatever is happening in the present. Our anger is usually out of proportion and an extreme overreaction. Why? It is an accumulation of pain that includes the present feeling on top of the past, unhealed emotion with many layers in between. We can be like an onion with numerous layers that have to be peeled back. We are unable to deal with the present as only the present, because the past has unconsciously been triggered. Because of abuse in my childhood, whenever I felt misused in the present I would overreact. Being unaware that what happened to me was abuse, I had no idea why, over and over again, I was reacting so strongly to feeling used. It wasn't until the reality of the abuse surfaced, and I was willing to face it as such, that my healing process began. Then I was finally able to make the connection that use is a form of abuse.

Let me share a common situation, one that I have certainly experienced. Suppose we are feeling embarrassed because we forgot an important appointment and someone we care about was hurt by it. A healthy response would be to acknowledge our failure and ask for forgiveness. Instead of being able to own our present failure, because of the build up of shame we might have been carrying throughout our lives, we instead get angry. We make excuses, want to hide, or blame others in an effort to cover our mistake instead of taking responsibility for it in a healthy way.

Facing the present feeling, in this case the shame of not being perfect, connecting it with the past, and then recognizing it was the same emotion in both cases, opens a door to healing. Jesus is able to connect with us there to bring healing because He also experienced similar emotions in His humanity. Jesus was falsely accused, rejected, shamed, and then betrayed by one of His friends, but when He stood before Pilate, He didn't defend Himself. "He made no reply, not even to a single charge..." (Matthew 27:12-14). Why? He knew who He was and on the deepest level of His being He could not be shamed (Isaiah 50:6,7). He wants to bring us to the place where we too can stand firm in the face of rejection, false accusation, and the shame that belongs to someone else and is not ours to carry. We might have grown up in an atmosphere of shame or rejection because of the unhealed wounds or addictions of our parents. Realize that this is not about blaming others. It is about simply feeling and acknowledging the emotions we felt at the time. That enables us to begin to welcome God into the pain to bring about healing. The next step, as we are ready, is to move toward heart forgiveness and release the one who wounded us in the past as well as the one in the present. Keep in mind that this is a process we cannot do alone, we must work it through with the Spirit's help, but since He is the Wonderful Counselor, He's there 24/7 to walk with us.

Displacing our Emotions

As children, another common strategy for dealing with pain or trauma is to displace a painful emotion and put it on someone or something else. For example, this might sound humorous, but as a child I displaced my fear and painful emotions by putting them on the dog. Every time I left the house, I constantly worried that the dog was afraid, lonely or feeling rejected. The truth was those were my feelings, not the dog's, and they put a tremendous burden on me as a young child to protect him. This can cause us to become fierce protectors of others, or caretakers of other's feelings in an unhealthy way. We might find ourselves trying to keep people happy so *they* don't experience the feelings we are trying to bury, thus becoming protectors of other's emotions, wanting to rescue them from any discomfort or inconvenience.

More significantly, we may tend to place our unhealed emotions on our children, trying to protect them from feeling that which we are afraid of experiencing ourselves. Our children's history is different from ours so they can experience the emotions differently than we do. For example, I placed my buried wound of rejection on my children. Because I had pain in that area, I assumed they did as well, but their years of growing up were different than mine. They might have pain too, but in different areas. Because of my false belief, I was tormented whenever they experienced not being chosen to play or not picked for some activity. Sadly, in my overreactions, I harmed them by trying to protect them from my pain. Our own unhealed emotions can cause us to either want to overprotect to keep our children from any pain or to distance ourselves emotionally from their genuine pain. We can do that by disregarding their emotions or telling them to just "get over it" when they are genuinely hurting.

An Atmosphere of Pain

Some of us might have grown up in an atmosphere of pain as opposed to having specific painful memories. I grew up in a home that contained an atmosphere of fear, rejection, and shame because of the pain my parents never faced. In order to survive feeling unwanted or not accepted, I built walls around myself, walls of anger and fear. I can see now that none of the rejection I experienced was purposefully directed at me, but because of their unhealed wounds, I experienced the overflow. For years, because of feeling overwhelmed with this fear of being rejected, I ran from any hint of possible rejection or abandonment. Anytime I thought someone might reject or replace me, I'd reject them first. For example, I'd watch their body language and read into their actions things that weren't really there just trying to keep myself safe and to never be surprised or caught off guard by their rejection. I lived continually on high alert because of not being able to be feeling of being exposed again. I'd flee if I thought rejection was coming, but none of this happened on a conscious level. I didn't purposely reject others, I didn't even know I was doing it for the most part, but as you can imagine it made a mess of any hope I might have had for healthy relationships. Sadly, that behavior was sabotaging the very thing I longed for, which of course was belonging and acceptance.

It wasn't until after many months of desperately crying out for freedom that God used a present day set-up in my life to trigger the horrendous pain of rejection that was hidden within me. It happened very unexpectedly at a family wedding in another state. Because of our late arrival, it quickly became apparent that all the tables had already been filled. A makeshift table was hurriedly set up to accommodate us, but we found ourselves sitting alone in a corner by the kitchen while everyone else was enjoying fellowship with others. It felt like I was on the outside looking in, just as I had felt my whole life. My husband appeared to be completely unaffected, but because God was answering my desperate prayer to set me free from whatever was keeping me imprisoned, He allowed my feelings of rejection from the past to finally surface. It caused me to overreact by feeling overcome with pain that came from the accumulated rejection of a lifetime. The rest of the reception was experienced with an overflow of anger and tears lurking just behind my eyes. I felt like I was having open-heart surgery without any anesthesia, but thankfully that experience finally surfaced the buried pain of my childhood and opened the door to being healed and set free.

As difficult as it was to face the pain I had carried within, I finally allowed Jesus to meet me there instead of closing it down again. Jesus was rejected and despised so He understood (Isaiah 53). That freed me as an exchange was made – His acceptance for my rejection. I finally had one relationship in which I would never know rejection because of what He also suffered for me. Jesus understood my pain and desired to meet me there with healing, bringing freedom and restoration to my soul. All that took a bit of time to walk all the way through, but until I could face the pain of the rejection I was carrying, I was trapped by it and, sadly, I was continually wounding others by trying to keep myself safe.

The Fullness of the Cross

Jesus' experience of rejection and abandonment by men is part of the fullness of the cross and what He suffered for us. The scriptures tell us He suffered in every way as we do (Hebrews 2:14-15 & Hebrews 4:14). Because Jesus suffered emotionally as well, He is able to understand the pain of a broken world, giving us His acceptance for our rejection, letting us know that we are accepted, wanted, and valued by Him. As I received His acceptance, much like we do in receiving salvation, a deep healing within began to take place. It happened in my broken heart and not just in my intellect. Jesus came to "bind up the brokenhearted and proclaim freedom for the captives" (Isaiah 61:1). In order to complete my healing, however, I had to finally release my anger and work toward forgiveness of those who had wounded me. That was not easy and it was a struggle to get there, but with His help I was finally able to do it. I was then able to say with Jesus' help, "Father forgive them for they do not know what they are doing" (Luke 23:34).

Remember that God is a God of light. Burying pain away, hiding it and covering it over leads to darkness. Healing takes place in the light. So as you identify the painful emotions, own them by feeling the pain, and embrace that little child within who carries that pain, Jesus the Healer is able to meet you there to bring restoration. The child inside then gets unstuck from the pain and he or she can restart the emotional growth process in that area to catch up with the rest of themselves. In doing that, integration begins within. "Give me an undivided heart that I may fear your name" (Psalm 86:11).

Through the years I've witnessed this process many times in

both myself and others.Once unstuck, the maturing can begin, sometimes happening relatively quickly, but it is still a growing process. It is joy to watch someone who was stuck in a particular childish way become integrated as the adult they are intended to be and begin to function differently.

Self-rejection and the Longing to be Accepted

Many of us have rejected the child within us because, as a child, we often felt dismissed or rejected by others. So many have developed a self-hatred or disdain for themselves. I know I did that for far too many years until I was finally able to see myself as God has always known and seen me, not who the accuser (Satan) said I was. We just do to ourselves what we felt others did to us. When those who were supposed to help us didn't see our pain or care for us in the way we needed, we often pushed that part of ourselves away as unacceptable. Now, as the buried emotions surface, you as the adult who knows Jesus can bring that crippled child to Him for healing.

When the disciples rejected the children and tried to keep them away from Him, Jesus rebuked the disciples and called the children to Himself for blessing (Matthew 19:13-15). In His love, Jesus, who is filled with compassion, wants to restore that little child within you who may have been trapped in pain for many years. We may pray for that healing, but not realize that we have a part to play in it also. We have to accept that child in order to bring him or her to Jesus for healing. When we first *see* that child in all his or her pain, we might realize we have been carrying a dislike for that little one. Sometimes the opposite happens and the child seems to *pull away* from the adult out of the fear of being rejected. This just shows how much we need to accept them because a rejection and separation has taken place without our realizing it. It can help at that point to pull out some old photos of yourself at various young ages. As you view the pictures, what feelings are provoked? Are you feeling warm toward that child or angry and rejecting?

All through my life I hated pictures of myself. I didn't like any part of me because, although I was not aware of it, I had judged myself as needy and pathetic. As thoughts of certain photos came to mind, I remembered myself with disdain. It wasn't until I came into some healing that I dared to pull them out and, to my surprise, I felt warm feelings toward that little one. She wasn't pathetic at all, she was sweet! Another person I know retrieved the photos of herself as a child, but refused to look at them, judging that child as worthless. Unfortunately, she was never willing to go any further with them and healing still has not come for her.

Have you longed for significant people to acknowledge you? Perhaps you wanted approval from an authority figure of some kind or desired a person of some importance to see you as significant. Maybe you didn't want approval and acceptance from everyone, but from the ones you have considered special. I did that for years, but why? It often reveals the little child within who never got that approval or acceptance from those who were put there by God to give it to them. That need is not coming from you as an adult, but from the child who has been left with their needs unmet. In fact, if we are to receive acceptance as an adult, the satisfaction never lasts if the child within is still wounded. It's the child who is still craving for someone to tell them they are okay and for someone to see them and acknowledge them. Fortunately, you can begin to cooperate with Jesus in giving acceptance to that little child within. How many men and women try to get that acceptance from the opposite sex and, even though they receive it, it's never enough. There is a huge empty place within that only Jesus can fill if you will cooperate by inviting Him into the pain.

Instead of trying to *pull* acknowledgement from a person who can't fill that hole within, try to allow the Spirit to take you back to that hungry little child. How old is he/she? What is he/she hungry for? See the child, feel what the child feels and bring that little one to Jesus. Remember that Jesus is the only one who can go back in time to that little child to fill his or her empty heart. Agree with Jesus over that child and let him or her know you also see that he/she is worth accepting. Then see if you can forgive those significant others who never acknowledged you.

It can be hard at first for us who are so bound by time, but since Jesus is outside of time as we know it, in faith allow your heart to go with Him to rescue that little child who has been lost and forgotten. Do it with your heart, not just your mind. Jesus, the scriptures tell us, came to seek and save that which is lost and that little one has been lost for a long time. Allow the One who is pictured in the scripture as the good Shepherd of the sheep to go after that little lamb within you who has been stuck in the briars and brambles all these years. That's His desire.

It is God who has given us our imagination, but the enemy has robbed us of it. For most of us, our imagination has been used more for picturing doom, gloom, and disaster than to *see* the scriptures. Our imagination has been given to us for a purpose and if we will use it with God's Spirit the way He intended we can flesh out the scriptures. We can begin to see, taste, and experience the scripture, entering into it to receive healing. We can *see* Jesus with the little children, tenderly embracing those His disciples tried to push away. We can *hear* Jesus rebuke the disciples and correct them regarding their view of the children. We can *experience* being one of those little children Jesus picks up on his lap and heals, blesses, restores. "Taste and see *that* the Lord is good" (Psalm 34:8).

Renurturing

Growth is a process, so it's not unusual for a person to identify with various ages along the way where the pain of life has kept them stuck. In that process, we can work with Jesus to nurture ourselves wherever we were not nurtured as children. That nurturing process looks different for each person, but if pain surfaces and you find, for example, that you have been stuck as a little girl at age five, then in order to connect with her you might find yourself wanting to go to the park and swing on the swings or color pictures of princesses in a coloring book. Do it! It's not foolish and it's for a very short time, but you are joining with Jesus in hearing her desires and nurturing her back to life.

Ask for God's help in discovering ways you can nurture that little one. What does he or she need? For some, writing a story about that lost little child helps them to listen to their voice, validate, and connect with them. Finding pictures of yourself as a child and really looking at them also helps. As you look into the child's eyes, what do you see? What is their body language telling you? What clues can you discover as to the pain they carry? What does he or she want to do? Do it and then allow Jesus to join you. I have spoken with grown men who have gotten in touch with that lost little child within and found themselves wanting to play with toy cars, trains or go out and play baseball. Allow yourself to do it and let Jesus play with you! If you have children of similar age, use that playtime with them to nourish your little child, too. Early on my journey, I discovered there was nurturing needed from when I was 18 months old. Fortunately, my grandson was about the same age at the time, so I just sat on the floor and played with him. Many years later, I look back on that time with warm feelings because, not only did I connect with him, but with my little child as well. Later, you might find yourself feeling more like a teenager and then finally as an adult of present age. It's a process, just like your growth was a process the first time around. The more we cooperate with Jesus in the process, the faster it goes.

Many Christians have confused self-nurture with selfishness or self-centeredness. When we have been wounded and stuck, nurture is necessary in the healing process. In nurturing, you are co-laboring with Jesus to give life and care back to that part of you who is still a child. Nurture is life giving and the scriptures describe God in many places as a nurturer. In life, there is a season to nurture a child and there is a season for that child to grow into maturity so he can walk as a responsible adult. If we are able to remain sensitive to the Spirit, we will move through the process with the goal of getting the part of us back that's been lost in order to be able to lay it down before Jesus. We can only give Him what we have. As long as parts of us remain buried in pain, we do not have that part of ourselves to give to either Jesus or to others.

The transition into adult responsibility is often hindered by being stuck as a little child who is still demanding to be taken care of by others. One young girl I know had been hindered from getting a job and taking adult responsibilities, but she never knew why. Finding that child and the pain he or she is carrying often begins the restoring process that eventually leads to them being able to take healthy responsibility for themselves. Sometimes we're able to make behavioral changes with a lot of effort, but how much better to have the axe laid to the root so our behavior changes from the inside out. Jesus informs us that our actions come from our hearts. When our hearts are wounded, our behavior is messed up, but as we allow Jesus to heal our broken hearts, new fruit begins to grow, good fruit that remains.

Many of us who have grown up in this imperfect, sin-filled, broken world have a number of such places that need restoring. You might not even know what they are until God allows a set-up or a trigger. Be willing to be aware of those triggers by inviting the Spirit to help you recognize them. Jesus is the Redeemer and wants to redeem all parts of us so that we can serve Him with our whole heart, soul, body, and spirit, as well as being able to love our neighbors as we love ourselves (Matthew 22:37-39).

Isn't it wonderful that God desires to work with us here? "May God himself, the God of peace, sanctify you through and through. May your whole spirit, soul and body be kept blameless at the coming of our Lord Jesus Christ" (1 Thessalonians 5:23).

Without realizing it, we are usually more in agreement with the enemy *against* that little child within than we are with Jesus who welcomes the children. In fact, He tells us that unless we become as a little child, we cannot even see the kingdom. Always keep in mind that, since restoration requires our co-laboring with Jesus, He needs us to work with Him on behalf of our little child and not against Him.

Listen to the words of your heart. Are they lining up more with the enemy against that little one or with Jesus who came to rescue him or her?

Questions to Ponder

In looking back at the little child who might be stuck within, how would you describe him/her? Notice the body language you see, attitude, etc.

What are your feelings toward the child?

How might you have judged the parts of you that you felt were unacceptable?

When you make a mistake what are the words you tell yourself?

What do you learn about how you see yourself from those words, especially if they are negative?

Is your self-talk more in agreement with a loving God or with Satan the accuser?

Assignment

Allow the Spirit to help you use your sanctified imagination to see Him as a shepherd, gathering that little one, carrying your little child close to His heart. Feel it. Stay there until you can experience that safety and acceptance.

Scriptures

In the coming days, work with these nurturing scriptures, allowing the Lord's warm, tender heart to reach into the heart of that little child within who was so hungry for love and acceptance.

"He tends His flock like a shepherd. He gathers the lambs in His arms and carries them close to His heart. He gently leads those that have young." Isaiah 40:11

"The Lord is with you, He is mighty to save. He will take great delight in you, He will quiet you with His love, He will rejoice over you with singing." Zephaniah 3:17

"It was I who taught Ephraim to walk, taking them by the arms; but they did not realize I led them with cords of human kindness, with ties of love. I lifted the yoke from their neck and bent down to feed them." Hosea 11:3,4

"As a mother comforts her child, so will I comfort you..." Isaiah 66:13

"In a desert land He found him, in a barren and howling waste; He guarded him as the apple of his eye, like an eagle that stirs up it's nest and hovers over it's young, that spreads its wings to catch them and carries on it's pinions." Deuteronomy 32:10-13

"Though my father and mother forsake me, the Lord will take me up." Psalm 27:10

"As a father has compassion on his children so the Lord has compassion on those who fear Him." Psalm 103:13

"A father to the fatherless, a defender of widows, is God... He sets the lonely in families." Psalm 68:5

"In all their distress he too was distressed...in his love and mercy he redeemed them; he lifted them up and carried them all the days of old." Isaiah 63:9

3
HEART AND HEAD SEPARATION

False Perceptions, Soul Wounding,
Overflow of Soul Pain into Our Bodies,
The Heart - Central to Life

"The mind takes in and processes information. But it remains for the most part, indifferent. It is your mind that tells you it is now 2:00 A.M. and your daughter has not returned, for the car is not in the driveway. Your heart wrestles with whether or not this is cause for worry. The heart lives in the far more bloody and magnificent realities of living and dying and loving and hating. That's why those who live from their minds are detached from life."
- John Eldredge, Waking the Dead

Emotions are simply the voice of our heart telling us what is going on within us and reveal to us what our heart is feeling at any particular time. When we don't listen to what we're feeling, we're unable to process those emotions, creating a separation between our hearts and heads. When we fail to listen to what our hearts are telling us, we stop living from the center of our being. Just today I met with someone who told me he was doing fine, at least that was what his head was telling him. However, recent reactions in several situations told a very different story. If, as Jesus said, it's out of our heart that our mouth speaks or our actions come, then what was going on in his heart that he was not acknowledging?

When our life begins to be lived from the head alone, it becomes a series of "shoulds," "oughts," and "have to's," often leading us to a passionless life of obligation and duty. We give others our hands, but seldom our hearts, and often develop shallow, dutiful relationships. In essence, we begin to lose our true selves and then live out of an image that might not even be ours, but often is the image others create for us. This can begin a life of performance and trying to please others, a life that originates from outside of the heart, causing us to lose our true selves.

Many people's hearts and heads have been moving on different journeys because they have learned to distance themselves from the true feelings of their hearts to avoid their painful emotions. For a number of us, that began in early childhood when there was no one to help us process painful feelings. Without our awareness, we developed a denial system to keep the pain from intruding. When our denial finally begins to be broken, the old painful feelings will often surface. That can cause us to feel the original emotions we experienced, sometimes going back to early childhood. This time, however, if we will allow ourselves to feel the emotions, they can be healed, freeing us to live more fully from our hearts.

To give you an example from my own life, I distanced myself from my heart and the pain of abandonment that was lodged there for over 30 years. I lived the life of a "good girl" in certain relationships and a "tough girl" in other more vulnerable ones, all the while trying to figure out what was required of me in order to be accepted. Both masks were designed to keep me feeling safe and free from feelings of abandonment, but neither came from my true heart. They were unconsciously crafted as a self-protective image to cover my pain. The sad truth is that even though I put much energy into performing well so I wouldn't be discarded, I felt isolated and lonely because no one was allowed near my heart, including myself. It was not until I faced the pain I had buried that healing could finally begin resulting in the relationships of the heart I had always longed for.

The scriptures reveal to us that having our heart alive and aware is most important. "Above all else, guard your heart, for it is the wellspring of life" (Proverbs 4:23). The NAS Bible translates the wellspring as the "springs of life," and the NKJV refers to "the issues of life" as coming from the heart. "For as he thinks in his heart, so is he" (Proverbs 23:7 NKJV). Just as it is necessary to care for our physical heart, it is essential to attend to our spiritual and emotional heart as well, for it is central to all else. As John Eldredge shares in his insightful book, *Waking the Dead*, "According to the Scriptures, the heart can be troubled, wounded, pierced, grieved, even broken." He goes on to say, "It can also be frightened, faint, cowardly, melt like wax." Our hearts are speaking to us, revealing what emotions need to be listened to if we are to work them through to a place of surrender to God in order to experience peace.

For a good portion of my life, there were other unhealed, neglected emotions besides rejection and abandonment buried in my heart that were causing me to live from outside of it, although I was unaware at the time of what I was doing. It became second nature for me to read people and situations so I could become whatever they wanted in order to gain acceptance. I actually became quite adept at pretending to be whatever others wanted me to be, all the while remaining lost and lonely deep inside. I was like the wind, blowing here and there, but never really anchored in who I was since my heart, the center of my being, had gotten lost so long before. I can remember numerous times when I pretended to like something or remain a part of something I really disliked in order to continue to be acceptable to the people I was with. How many teens get caught in this and find themselves trapped into doing things they know are wrong just to continue to have a place of belonging? Because of the fear I carried that I would be abandoned, I, along with so many others, lived a life of what I believed was acceptable and necessary pretense. Sadly, I was actually selling my soul for the illusion of acceptance.

To discover the buried feelings locked in our hearts is not to say that we are to *live* out of our emotions for that would be disastrous; many have gotten shipwrecked that way. However, our feelings tell us what our heart is experiencing and whether it is stressed out, feeling rejected, overwhelmed, fearful, guilty, sad, lonely, disappointed or maybe even angry, so that we can care for it and tend to that which needs changing by working through those painful emotions. Doing so enables us to arrive at a healthy, peaceful, forgiving place, for it is also from the heart that forgiveness needs to flow. Our hearts can also tell us that we feel joyful, restful, thankful, or peaceful, as well as a multitude of other positive emotions. When we block the negative feelings, we unfortunately don't fully enjoy the positive ones either, and we just feel dull or dead inside. Emotions are to be felt and accepted as our own so that they can be worked through and released with the help of the Spirit of God. One of the Holy Spirit's names is the Helper and another is the Counselor; He is there with us 24/7 so we never have to be left alone with this task.

Jesus experienced painful emotions, too, and had to work them through just as we do. We see an example of this when Jesus heard the news of the death of John the Baptist. His response was to withdraw alone to a solitary place (Matthew 14:13). When told of Lazarus' death, Jesus wept (John 11:35). His response was very human, even though a short time later, He raised Lazarus from the dead. How many times in the gospels do we see Him being rejected and spoken falsely about? He truly understands the pain we go through so is able to identify with us there to bring healing to our broken hearts.

"Since the children have flesh and blood, he too shared in their humanity so that by his death he might destroy him who has the power of death – that is the devil and free those who all their lives were held in slavery by their fear of death… For this reason, he had to be made like his brothers in every way, in order that he might become a merciful and faithful high priest… Because he himself suffered when he was tempted, he is able to help those who are being tempted." (Hebrews 2:14-17)

Let's take a moment and look at that "fear of death" passage. We are so thankful that the actual fear of death and the fear of what happens thereafter are removed through our true understanding of salvation. However, I believe if we consider the fear of death more broadly, we can see how it affects our day-to-day living. Could it also refer to the *fear of the death* of a relationship, the *fear of the death* of our acceptance if we don't perform perfectly, the *fear of the death* of being included if we don't please people, causing us to fear being abandoned and the horror of being left all alone?

For years the *fear of death* of relationship and being left all alone tormented me even though the fear of literal death did not. Just the thought of being alone transported me back to the isolation and loneliness of my childhood. As a child, I felt emotionally abandoned even though I always had a family there to care for my physical needs. Along with the fear of abandonment came the shame of feeling that I wasn't enough in anyone's eyes to be wanted, accepted, and enjoyed. The shame I carried, lodged deep within my heart, became a secret I kept not only from others' eyes, but also from my own through denial.

When we have experienced hurtful circumstances as children and when there was no one there to help us through them, we might have become trapped alone in our pain. I remember experiencing a great deal of pain just because of a teasing comment my father made about me when I was 5 or 6 years old. My grandmother told my dad I looked just like him and his comment was that, if he looked like me, he would have killed himself! You can imagine the belief I developed about myself through that careless comment. The lie I believed told me I was ugly, deformed, and deserving to be hidden away from the eyes of others. Sadly, that belief remained within me until the shame I carried surfaced at age 50, allowing me to finally see the truth in order to receive healing. Until then I hated everything about myself. Children don't have the ability to distinguish teasing from reality, so whatever is said can be absorbed into the child as truth, especially when they are already feeling unloved and rejected. Jesus experienced the same emotions we have, but overcame them through the cross. If we invite Him, Jesus will meet us in our pain with healing, just as He does in releasing forgiveness to us through salvation. That opens the door to a new intimacy with Him and begins the process of restoring what the enemy has stolen.

When we don't listen to our emotions, disregarding them as unimportant and stuffing them down inside, they will too often come forth in inappropriate ways and at unexpected times. It is similar to a beach ball being held under the water. As long as we keep pressure on it, the ball remains hidden, but as soon as we let go, it surfaces with force. Our feelings may even come out as displaced emotions. An example of that might be when you yell at your children out of the frustration you feel toward your spouse or your job. Not being able to talk back, our children then begin to take their anger out on each other or on the dog! A child fearful of what is going on at home might act out their frustrations at school or pick on neighborhood kids, even becoming a bully.

At another time, un-faced emotions might come out in our dreams and, if we still do not listen to what we are feeling deep within us, our dreams can recur over and over or even become nightmares. Dreams can simply reveal to us what is going on within us that we are not acknowledging. They use symbolic language to speak to us so, when we begin to pay attention and understand what they are speaking, our dreams can be wonderful counselors, revealing the struggles of our hearts. A great source for gaining a deeper understanding of dreams and how to interpret them is Barbie L. Breathitt's book, *Dream Encounters: Seeing Your Destiny from God's Perspective.*

There are usually two extremes we fall into with our feelings and neither one is healthy. If we picture the healing journey as a road, then the ditch on one side is that we ignore and push our emotions away, stuffing them down inside and locking them in a closet. In the ditch on the other side of the road, we find ourselves wounding others because of allowing our emotions to rule us. In that case, we are enslaved by our emotions instead of simply listening to what they are telling us, processing those feelings with the help of the Holy Spirit, and choosing what we will do about what they reveal. When we are unable to make a good choice or we feel stuck, it's often because that same emotion from the past has not been healed. Because of the unhealed wound, our freedom to choose how to handle the current situation is limited and we feel tormented, driven or ruled by the emotion. We are not free to make logical choices. We know it and instead find ourselves reacting emotionally. Our healing simply gives us back the freedom to choose wisely, making room for God-given wisdom.

I've known numerous women who struggle with tears erupting at inappropriate times, often being unable to control them. When you suggest that it would be helpful to get in touch with their buried tears by having a good cry so the grief could be released, the immediate response is, "I'm afraid if I start crying, I'll never be able to stop." If we experienced significant losses while we were growing up, and there was no one to help us grieve those losses, our tears can remain buried within. As children we are often told not to cry or even shamed for being a crybaby, so the tears are stuffed down within us where they remain until triggered in the present.

Those triggered tears will stop when they are fully released. Tears often have words connected to them as well so it can be helpful to get in touch with the words and express them out loud, listening to what they are telling you. Your tears might have words like, "No one has ever wanted to really see or know me," or "I feel alone, forsaken." Those are just two examples of the emotional words of tears, but they could be telling you many things about how your heart is feeling if you are willing to listen. We can't release what we've never faced so it's important to acknowledge the emotions that have been locked up within. There is a wonderful picture in the Bible of God collecting our tears in a bottle (Psalm 56:8 NKJV). Because we are so precious to Him, the sorrow that caused our tears is never disregarded or minimized. Sometimes when our tears have been suppressed for many years, they will even become a wail. That just shows the depth of anguish that has been buried within.

I had that experience. I hadn't allowed myself to cry for many years so, when a painful circumstance would arise, I just kept suppressing the tears by denying my hurt. The lie I told myself was, "That doesn't bother me." Of course it bothered me deeply, but I wouldn't allow myself to acknowledge or feel it. For example, when I felt hurt by something my husband or another person said, my automatic response was to put another brick over my heart and allow resentment to build toward that person. While it deadened my pain on the surface, the hurt was pushed deeper within and then was unable to be released. If I had owned the hurt, I could have allowed myself to feel the sadness, cry if necessary, forgive the person and move on.

Since I never allowed the tears at the time, when they finally broke free in a safe atmosphere they came out with wails from the deepest part of my being. I was shocked! My first thought was, "Who is that?" Then I realized the wails were coming from me! As I finally allowed Him, Jesus was able to meet me there with comfort because He is a "man of sorrows and familiar with suffering" (Isaiah 53:3).

The ditch on the other side of the road can be seen when un-faced emotions erupt in the form of suppressed rage that usually hurts others. Unfortunately, the people harmed most by our explosiveness are usually those that are closest and ones we care deeply about. Many times a present-day happening triggers an uncontrollable angry reaction. Where did that come from? Often it came from layer upon layer of buried frustration or anger from the past. It came from anger that was never owned and released and might have gone back as far as early childhood, but remained hidden. For some it can be tied to a horrific circumstance or for others a continual atmosphere of injustice. This is especially true for anyone who had abuse of any kind in their background. The anger buried within from that abuse can become a river of rage inside, leaking out in many ways like depression, explosiveness or even in physical ailments. Through that we can also develop false beliefs about ourselves.

How much better it is to allow the Spirit to bring to light the lies we have believed about ourselves, as well as our past frustration or anger. With the help of the Spirit, false beliefs can be faced, our wounds healed, and emotions finally released by forgiving the ones who hurt us. Entering that process frees us to respond to the present appropriately instead of reacting out of the buried emotion of the past, which can cause uncontrolled explosions or overreactions. For some, the unacknowledged anger goes underground and instead comes out as depression. Anger that is not faced as anger, but is locked inside can cause a further shutdown of emotions, resulting in depression.

I lived with low-grade depression all my life and never knew it, as did my father before me. It was not until I began to face my buried anger and recognize the powerlessness I was feeling in various situations, especially those regarding losses, that the depression lifted. I had to face my anger as anger instead of trying to minimize it, so it could be released. Doing that enabled me to feel the disappointed longings the anger was covering. Through the years, I desired many things that never happened. Instead of facing the disappointments and grieving them, I just shut down inside and that resulted in depression. Whenever I didn't recognize the anger being provoked in me, I would begin to feel depressed. So using that as a red flag, I stopped and asked the Spirit to show me what I was angry about any time I began to feel depressed. Once I faced and released the anger, disappointment and the loss it covered, my depression would go away.

Another example of buried emotions sabotaging our present life can be seen in the area of rejection. To give you another example from my own life, because of the rejection I experienced as a child, I *read rejection* into almost every encounter. I *saw rejection* where there was no rejection and sadly that continued to harm my relationships in the present. Our emotions don't always have to come from one particular trauma, but as in my case, they came from growing up in an *atmosphere* of rejection which stemmed from my parents' own lifetime of unhealed rejection.

There is often a lie we have believed at the core of our being, a false belief that entered through the painful circumstances of our past. I had a number of lies at my core. One particular lie was that I was "rejectable," and since I believed it as if it were truth, I lived out of it. Scripture calls Satan the "father of lies." He has access to any lie within us, so our agreement with a lie becomes a place for him to hook us with fear and torment. By recognizing the lie and getting out of agreement with it, we close the access the enemy has to that place. Doing this allows the Spirit of Truth to come in with healing and peace as we begin the process of living out of God's truth instead of the lie or our false perception of the truth. Jesus said, "…the prince of this world is coming. He has no hold on me." (John 14:30) There was no place within Jesus for Satan to hook Him. There was no darkness within Him. False beliefs and lies are darkness.

Our Perceptions

Let's talk for a minute about perceptions. What we perceive as truth when we're children is *truth to us* even though it might be a *false perception* and not factual at all. It is not enough just to tell someone they believe a lie, because they still have painful emotions surrounding their perception. For example, let's look again at the lie I believed that said I was rejectable; that lie was truth to me because of how I interpreted what I experienced. It wasn't until I allowed myself to feel the rejection the little girl within me originally felt and invited Jesus to meet me there with healing that I was able to finally see it was a lie. Seeing that moved me forward on the road toward forgiving my father. The truth was that because rejection is often passed on, and my father experienced rejection that he never faced, his way of expressing love was often twisted, coming out in the form of cruel teasing. Since children are not always able to distinguish between teasing and truth, they can be hurt deeply, especially when they are starving for acceptance. Through healing, I was finally able to recognize that my father had indeed loved me, but his own fear and rejection had prevented him from expressing it in a healthy manner. It is not until the painful emotions are allowed to surface, looked at without judgment, and connected to whatever pain the lie we believe seems to evoke in us, that healing by receiving God's truth can replace the false belief. We must have our own emotions healed so that we don't pass the pain on to our children and they, in turn, to their children.

If a child learns at an early age, as I did, that it's not safe to trust people because they hurt you, a belief can be developed deep within that says, "Don't trust, for if you do, you know you'll be destroyed." That belief for me became a secret inner vow that created fear and the need to control. With the fear to trust, no matter how much scripture to the contrary we might learn about how much God loves us and how much we love God, we will find it extremely difficult to surrender our whole heart to Him. It can also affect our willingness to be open-hearted with others. The vow we made sabotages our ability to trust again. We will try hard to trust, perhaps doing it for a short while, but it will never seem to last for long.

The Wounding Happens in Our Soul

What do our emotions tell us? For one thing they tell us what we believe on a very deep level in our hearts. Strange as it may seem, they also communicate just how fully we *trust God*. How often we glibly say, "Oh, I trust God," and we do in our heads, but our emotions are telling a very different story. Deep within our hearts, we are filled with anxiety, fear or even anger. Our head believes and trusts, but our hearts are living out of another belief system entirely so that we are not united within ourselves, spirit, soul, body. We find ourselves at odds within ourselves, but sadly we often refuse to admit it. Anger at God might be lodged in our hearts because of the circumstances He either has allowed or is allowing to happen to us. Until we honestly face that anger, we can't resolve it and God continues to feel far away. Since He knows us fully, we might as well face our anger since it has never really been hidden from Him anyway.

As humans, we are made up of spirit, soul, and body. When we come to Jesus our spirits come alive and love the Lord, however, through the painful circumstances and difficulties of life, our souls have been wounded, sometimes many times over. Our souls are made up of our mind, our will, and our emotions. Since the wounds of life affect our emotions, until that buried pain is healed it is very difficult to truly trust God deeply in the areas in which we have been hurt. We can find this playing out in areas like finances or relationships when there was no security in the home growing up. There will be other areas in which we have no trouble trusting Him at all because no wounding has occurred there.

One area in which it was very difficult for me to trust God was when something would end; I would have little faith or trust there would ever be something good again to replace it. My automatic response was to feel hopeless. Because I struggled with it so often, my friends began to mention it. It wasn't until I seriously asked God why, that He showed me. As a child, I felt the pain of things being taken from me, but they were rarely replaced with something else that was good, causing in me the need to hold onto everything. In fact, I was even disciplined with the fear of loss if I didn't behave. Facing the fear of that little girl within made a way for Jesus to meet me there, enabling me to forgive the ones responsible for my pain. Finally, there was room for God to speak His truth into my heart. The first thing He did was to quote only a portion of John 3:16 by saying, "God so loved the world that He gave…" It was an awakening moment, and for the first time in my life, my heart realized that God is a giver, not a taker. When He does take, there is a purpose we don't understand, but He always gives again because that's His nature.

Having unhealed wounds in our soul will also make it more difficult for us to have our will line up with God's will in the particular area that was hurt. For instance, after allowing God to heal my wound of abandonment and then dealing with the anger that surrounded it, I was able to speak up in a much bolder way when God asked me to. Prior to that, even though I knew He was asking me to share, I couldn't because of my fear of man's rejection and abandonment. My will wanted to be obedient to what He asked, but the old fear paralyzed me. In other areas that have not been wounded, surrendering our will to His won't be such a battle because there is far less anxiety. We are not stuck in all of our emotions, but only in the ones that connect to our buried pain. When we are having trouble submitting our will to His and cannot come to a place of peace, that is another red flag to alert us to a need for healing.

God longs for us to love Him with our whole heart, our whole soul, and with our whole mind, but sadly we are unable to do that fully until restoration takes place within. "May God himself, the God of peace, sanctify you through and through. May your whole spirit, soul, and body be kept blameless at the coming of our Lord Jesus Christ. The one who calls you is faithful and He will do it." (1 Thessalonians 5:23, 24) He has provided for our restoration through the cross, but it takes our cooperation with Him to complete the process in our everyday living. "Continue to work out your salvation with fear and trembling, for it is God who works in you to will and to act according to His good purpose" (Philippians 2:12, 13).

Do you ever wonder why you can read of God's love and acceptance and believe it's true for others, but still have trouble believing those words are true for you? Your head believes the truth and you know the scriptures say so, but somehow that truth never gets deep within you and never quite lasts, at least not for long. Your head believes, but your emotions inside are telling you something very different. Why? When we didn't feel valued, accepted or enjoyed as children, we will have a hard time resting in the truth that we are enjoyable and acceptable even to God.

If abuse or betrayal of any kind was involved, we will be affected in our day-to-day living whether we are aware of it or not. Until the lies and false beliefs that those experiences *taught* us are brought to the light, along with the surrounding pain, we are often robbed of the joy and peace that allow us to enjoy God's love and acceptance. Instead, it can leave us striving, performing, and feeling like we will never measure up to the standard and still trying to earn our acceptance. It can also cause us to want to hide those parts of ourselves that we have judged as inadequate or shameful.

Do you ever struggle with criticizing and judging others? Have you condemned yourself for it and felt guilty? I struggled with judgment and criticism for many years and hated being like that. So many times I would come away from a situation with a judging attitude if someone didn't measure up to the standard I set, but even while doing it, I hated myself for judging them. I would repent and ask for forgiveness over and over because I didn't want to be critical. I wanted to love and accept others, but until I finally began to accept myself, that was impossible for me. The root of a critical spirit can be a lack of self-love, or even self-hatred in extreme cases, that comes out of those unhealed wounds. The scripture tells us that we love others as we love ourselves. When we don't experience the true self-love and acceptance that comes from God's love for us, it becomes impossible to really love and accept others, especially when they don't measure up to our standard. We're just judging them in the same way we're judging ourselves –as insufficient and not measuring up.

The answer is not more self-condemnation or trying harder to love, which is what we usually do, but instead allowing that criticism to lead us to Jesus for healing of our lack of self-love. Instead of beating ourselves up for a critical spirit, we can see it as a symptom revealing that we might never have truly loved ourselves on a deep heart level by accepting the love God has for us just the way we are. We might have believed it in our head, but Jesus reveals that it is "…out of the overflow of the heart, the mouth speaks" (Matthew 12:34). In that case, our criticism is trying to tell us something. It is telling us there is a wound in the heart that is keeping us from truly loving ourselves, others, and often God as well, at least at the deepest level of the heart.

How do we love? We love because Jesus first loved us (1 John 4:19). From that we learn that love begins with God and not with us. When our hearts do not believe that we are loved by God just the way we are though we don't deserve it, and if we are unable to agree with God about ourselves by showing ourselves love, we will be unable to really love others. We might cover it over and try to be nice, but still have self-judgment and criticism in our hearts that will eventually come out of our mouths toward others. We might try to put a lid on it and attempt to change our behavior, but behavioral change never lasts for long if our hearts still believe a lie about ourselves. Our actions will spring from our hearts whether our hearts are healed or unhealed. When healed, the fruit will be different. How sad it is that, as Christians, we are often more in agreement against ourselves with the accuser of the brethren, as Satan is called, than we are with the Spirit of Truth who loves, accepts, and enjoys us.

Deep inside there is often a shame belief fearing that if we ever stop striving to prove we're acceptable through whatever means we might be using to cover ourselves, such as work, service or performance of some kind, we will be found insufficient and unacceptable. When I struggled with my addiction to people's approval, I feared that if I ever stopped trying to be all things to all people, they would throw me away. That drove me to continually try to make people happy with me. I could never rest. For some, a false belief causes them to go the opposite way so they never try very hard at anything, living far beneath who they really are because of the fear of failure or of being exposed as inadequate. Deep within we can be tormented with the fear of being seen as not having what it takes. We often see ourselves as a failure because we have failed at *some* things. The truth is that none of us does all things well - we're not supposed to. We all have strengths and weaknesses. Yet our fears of failure often reveal a deep root of illegitimate or false shame, which we will spend more time exploring in a later chapter. There are also times when, even though we are responsible people, the circumstances of life will make us appear irresponsible and, if that shame belief is there, we might feel like a failure and experience torment.

When we have been deeply hurt we can be crippled and not know why. Our spirits know how to soar and when we're in a spiritual atmosphere we might find ourselves doing very well, but it never seems to last for long. Shortly afterward we find ourselves back in the pit. To compensate, we might try harder spiritually, pushing the feelings away by going to more meetings, reading the Bible more, praying more or listening to more worship music. Again, that may work for a short time, but we will never feel really free and whole until the axe gets to the root of the problem. Good roots or beliefs produce good fruit and twisted roots or false beliefs produce bad fruit (Matthew 7:17). Jesus encourages us to bear good fruit that remains, which is why we need to work with Him in putting the axe to the root of any false belief we might be living from (John 15:16).

Sadly, Christians don't usually discuss areas like this because there can be an accompanying feeling that says, "There's something wrong with me," and we believe the lie that says, "No one else is like this." As we believe those words, the false shame becomes even greater and the covering over our hearts gets put more firmly in place causing us to hide even from ourselves, fearing we're unacceptable on the deepest level.

The false shame belief often throws us into the journey of living life from outside of our hearts. We try to do and say the right things, we work harder to please others to get their acceptance, we try to create the right image, and obtain what we believe is necessary to look successful, but deep within when we finally get quiet, we know it's never enough. So we just try harder, stress ourselves more or try to hold it all together more fiercely. If we are to be truly honest deep within, we are never really at rest or at peace and our soul is not satisfied. Sadly, that performance lifestyle might be present regardless of whether we are in the church or in the world.

Our Bodies

If we continue to bury our feelings, they can begin to come out in our bodies wherever the weakest place might be. We might begin to get headaches, backaches, skin rashes, frequent colds, flu or a weakened immune system that brings on countless other ailments. It's not that the symptoms aren't real, they are in fact very real, but are often induced by the emotions we have not allowed ourselves to feel. Un-faced guilty feelings also can come out in body sickness over time, as we see in Psalm 32. If you think your buried feelings might be surfacing in body ailments and want more understanding, I recommend you read Rebecca Maisenbacher's book, "If I'm Healed By His Stripes, Then Why Do I Still Hurt?" especially chapter 15. Rebecca's book is available through The Covenant Center (www.thecovenantcenter.com) and does an excellent job of compiling research on the emotion/body connection. The longer we live with those painful emotions pushed down within, the more our bodies are affected in numerous ways. We might even use emotional eating to feed our hungry hearts or be pulled in ways to avoid lovingly caring for ourselves, our families, our homes or our belongings.

I had many minor ailments that went away as I faced my emotional pain and allowed God to heal my buried emotions. As a child, I got a cold every time I felt helpless and overwhelmed with life. I didn't consciously choose to get sick, it just happened. It was an unconscious way of not facing those particular emotions, but it did several things for me without my awareness. It gave me a reprieve from life, freedom from anyone's expectations of me, and it gave me some much needed attention that I was starved for. Actually, it wasn't even healthy attention; it was sympathy, which only served to reinforce my already entrenched victim mentality. In my early adult life, I developed the flu every Christmas season. As a child, Christmas was always a painful holiday for me, so without realizing it, I found a way to avoid Christmas and the emotional pain it caused by having physical pain to deal with. I had very real flu with very real symptoms, but I believe my emotional state weakened my immunity and, without realizing it, I *welcomed* a reprieve. I *welcomed* the flu as an acceptable escape from life for a while. As I got older and began to face my buried emotions to get healing from them, my health improved dramatically in countless ways. In fact, I was no longer focusing on my body at all, I was just expecting it to function the way God designed it to flow. When we are in harmony within, there is a flow of life and renewed energy resulting in new strength, peace, and rest. We accomplish much and enjoy more because we are connected with God as well as with our own hearts, resulting in a sense of well-being.

So many people tell me they feel divided or separated inside, sometimes using phrases like, "I'm not feeling whole inside," or "I don't feel unified within." When deeply wounded emotionally and not knowing what to do with the pain, a child will often separate from the hurt by locking that particular feeling away. When those feelings get walled off, the rest of their life keeps growing, however, a separation is caused within and there is no longer unification on the inside. Without realizing it, they have separated themselves from the part that carries the pain. Just today I met with a woman who lost most of her positive memories and emotions by separating from her painful childhood feelings. Since there was no one there to help her through the pain, that's how she survived. Now in order to get back the positive memories and emotions, she must face the hurtful ones as well. The rest of her life had developed, she was intelligent and successful in her job, but she remained separated from a crucial part of herself. We have a beautiful picture of Jesus standing at the door and knocking (Revelation 3:20). We need to invite Him wholeheartedly into the pain because Jesus came to bind up the brokenhearted and to set the captives free (Isaiah 61:1).

As their healing progresses, I often hear words like, "I feel more whole, I feel like I am getting substance, I'm becoming more solid" or "I feel more together inside." Personally, I no longer feel like that feather blowing in the wind and never landing anywhere,

but instead I feel more like a person of substance who
solid, and connected inside. It has been a journey to g
know there is more unification still to come, but it feels wonderful
just to begin to finally discover and live life from my heart as *me*.

"Give me an undivided heart that I might fear your name."
(Psalm 86:11)

---

*Please Lord, give me a heart that's no longer divided, but
instead I desire that my heart and head flow together in
one accord and in one purpose – your purpose for me.
Help me to be in harmony – spirit, soul and body – so I
can love you with all my soul, all my heart, and all my
strength. Thank you!*

The Heart, Central to Life

---

*"Life is a journey of the heart that requires the mind -
not the other way around."*
*"Caring for our own hearts isn't selfishness,
it's how we begin to love."*
*"Caring for your heart is how you protect your
relationship with God."*
*- John Eldredge, The Journey of Desire and
Waking the Dead*

True life has to be lived from the heart. If we distance ourselves
from that deepest part, we have no truly meaningful life at all
even though on the outside we do it all well and are admired by
many. We learn from the world around us to value everything but
our own hearts. The distance we have created within is often so
great that many times we don't realize we've gotten lost or, if
we do, how to get ourselves reconnected. It is through the heart

we connect with God, ourselves and others on an intimate level. When we feel disconnected and separated or if God feels far off, it's not God we've lost connection with, it's our own heart. As soon as we reconnect with our heart, we are able to sense God's presence again waiting for us.

Just this week I had an example of this. After returning from a wonderful, action-packed vacation that was great fun, but left no time to rest and connect with my heart, I hit the ground running as soon as I arrived home. Everything had backed up and that caused me to play catch-up. Day by day, I was feeling more and more weary, dreading doing the same things all over again the next day. My mind was not focused. My usual wonderful connecting time with God's heart seemed distant. I was wearing out, spirit, soul, and body. What happened? The answer is I lost touch with my own heart. As I finally allowed myself to listen to what my heart was saying, remaining still long enough to feel, and then to share it all with God in my writings to Him, I immediately felt a reconnection with myself as well as with God. Along with that came renewed vigor and the energy to enter the new day with joy in my heart. Amazingly, the whole process took very little time.

Connecting with God through writing enables us to by-pass our mind and go straight to the heart. I never write Him from my head, but always from my innermost being, my heart. I'm often amazed at what I find there and how it differs from what my mind is thinking. That's why worship or music can touch us so deeply. That, too, often by-passes our mind and goes directly to the heart. A movie or a story can do the same, as well as art, a sunset, or being in nature by the ocean, a stream or waterfall. The beauty of nature feeds our hungry heart and connects us with the true Creator of it all. I can't encourage you enough to begin to do more of the things that feed your heart, for to lose heart is to lose everything that matters. Driving home from a long trip recently, I was extremely weary, but as I entered central Florida, the sunset was incredible. There were powerful dark storm clouds across the horizon, but peeking out from behind them was bright sunlight, making the contrast incredible! As I allowed God to speak to my heart through them, I felt a new strength enter into my soul. They were a picture of the darkness that can be on the horizon of our lives, but if we will look up, we can see the "Sun of Righteousness" with healing in His wings (Malachi 4:2).

Since it is also on the heart level that we truly connect with others, when we cover our hearts our relationships are often superficial. They can be enjoyable, but usually not deeply satisfying. We long to be truly known and still accepted with all the good, bad, and ugly. The thought of having any bad or ugly might cause a strong reaction in you because that's the part we usually try to hide from others, if not also from ourselves. For years I was convinced that if people ever really knew me, they would throw me away. The lie said I had to be perfect in order to be accepted, which of course was why I wore a mask. A funny thing happened though, as I began to be honestly me without the image, people began to love me instead of just having admiration. Some were a bit shocked as they began to realize all my imperfections, but instead of throwing me away, most could relate and actually drew closer. At the same time, it also began to open a door for them to honestly view their own hearts. That, in turn, brings forth a whole new relationship with God because then we don't have to hide ourselves from Him either, realizing that He has known us all along. Even while knowing all the things we haven't acknowledged about ourselves, some that are not too pretty, He has always accepted us.

As we begin to live life on the heart level, we also begin to recognize our motivations and the things that have often driven us without our awareness. "All a man's ways seem innocent to him, but motives are weighed by the Lord" (Proverbs 16:2). Or similarly, "All a man's ways seem right to him, but the Lord weighs the heart" (Proverbs 21:2). Until we connect with our own hearts, we usually don't recognize our motivations so many times we might be doing the right things, but for the wrong reasons. As we honestly begin to connect with our own hearts, there is a purification of our motives that begins to happen enabling us to co-labor with God for His purposes and not just for our own.

"A wise man's heart guides his mouth, and his lips promote instruction" (Proverbs 16:23).

Connecting with our hearts also opens the door to awaken desire and allows our dreams to come alive again. We begin to connect with our passions and the deepest longings of our hearts. In his book, *The Journey of Desire*, John Eldredge states, "We abandon the most important journey of our lives when we abandon desire. We leave our hearts by the side of the road and head off in the direction of fitting in, getting by, being productive, what have you." Our longings, dreams, and desires have gotten thwarted many times over, so through the years we've learned to bury them, considering them unimportant since it has seemed futile to desire deeply. We learned to live our lives from outside our hearts, offering our hands instead of our hearts, serving others, but sadly the deepest part of us remains buried. Then we wonder why we have no passion for anything, including God. We feel dull. We exist, but rarely live. In his book *Shattered Dreams*, Larry Crabb speaks of desire, "We kill desire in an effort to escape pain, then wonder why we don't enjoy God."

God has put dreams within our hearts; unique dreams and desires that fit us and connect with who we have been created to be. We might have misinterpreted them or tried to fulfill them ourselves. We might have gotten disappointed and abandoned those dreams and desires, but they still hold a key to who we really are and the purposes we've been created to fulfill.

Questions to Ponder

If you feel a separation inside, how would you describe it?

Can you describe some times when double-mindedness has been a problem?

When you think of God, what is your head telling you about Him?

Now listen to the fears and disappointments of your heart, what are they telling you about God?

List the areas in which you struggle, areas like decision-making, criticism, accepting yourself, striving, performing well, etc. Ask God to show you where they come from.

Assignment

Most of us have to start with superficial longings before we can even get to the deeply buried desires. Make a list of your dreams, desires, and longings.

Psalm 139 tells us that God has searched us and knows us. He has always known us even before our birth. So He alone knows the real you and desires to reveal you to you, the one He has always loved and enjoyed. Jesus stands at the door of your heart, knocking, waiting to meet with you there. Jesus came to restore you to His original intent, before the robbery from a broken world happened.

Begin to ask Him to reveal to you who you really are and what you desire. Then remain open and alert to clues as to what excites you and brings you life. When you get them, write them down because the enemy will try to erase them from your mind.

Scripture

"O Lord, you have searched me and you know me." Psalm 139:1

4
HIDDEN BEHIND A MASK

Who am I Really?

"And we, who with unveiled faces all reflect the Lord's glory, are being transformed into his likeness with ever-increasing glory, which comes from the Lord, who is the Spirit." 2 Corinthians 3:18

I remember taking a particular personality quiz many years ago. At the time, I was unaware that I was taking the test through my mask or false self. Retaking that same quiz years later after having cooperated with God in some emotional healing, the difference was amazing. The mask we wear serves a purpose: it hides the real us, the one we judge as not acceptable and it is a way of protecting our hearts from further shame, rejection, and pain. We may have begun to live out of that false self while we were still children because who we really were didn't seem to be enough. In some cases, who we were felt downright rejected so we abandoned our true self and covered it over with a mask. We might actually function quite acceptably through the mask, but sadly there isn't the full release of joy, peace, passion, and fullness of life as there is when living from our true hearts. Living from the heart is more than functioning or existing it's living and it enables us to begin the journey of fulfilling the purposes for which we were created. "The heart is the wellspring of life" and we are warned to watch over it carefully (Proverbs 4:23). When we don't and we bury our hearts under a mask, we are not truly who we are created to be.

At a very young age, because of the way I interpreted my life and viewed myself, I hid behind a mask of my own making. I became quite adept at figuring out who the person I was with wanted me to be and accommodating them. I recall a time at around six years of age when all the neighborhood kids were playing in a very muddy park that was being built and got their hands filthy. Because they didn't want to go home like that and get in trouble, I invited them to wash their hands in the newly installed drinking fountain and dry them on my dress. I might get reprimanded, but it was worth it if that would earn me some acceptance with the kids I longed to have include me. I was like a chameleon, continually changing colors to fit into my environment. My unspoken plea was, "Please see me and accept me, I'll be whoever you want. Just don't throw me away!" The real me had been buried as unacceptable years before. I didn't even know my true self or, if I ever did, that person had been lost and forgotten. I did know this for sure, I didn't like her because she didn't seem acceptable and I had judged her as pathetic for even desiring acceptance. In fact, I didn't like anything about her. Her name, her face, her personality; I had judged it all.

As a young child I would often go into my father's flower garden when it was blooming to rename myself through the flowers, so I became Petunia, Zinnia, or Morning Glory, anything that seemed pretty and other than who I believed myself to be. It became a standard joke with the neighbors often asking me, "And what is your name today?" Although I didn't know it at the time, a name connects to our identity. My own name and identity always felt ugly and shameful. Name calling can be so painful because it connects to the deepest part of our being. God promises us a new name, and a new identity to replace our shame (Isaiah 62:2-5).

People around us can even encourage the use of our mask because it can serve them. One woman I helped was always available for anything the church ever needed, even doing jobs that were definitely not along the lines of her particular gifts. Sadly, she resented those who used her, but at the same time it gave her a false identity since she believed they *needed* her help. How would they ever get along without her? The church encouraged her, even exalted her at times because she was always there for them, but unfortunately they never bothered to find out what might have been driving her service so they could really help her. Sometimes, the mask a person wears is that of a pleaser and they cover themselves by serving others. Serving from that motivation, though, is servitude instead of servant hood. That mask can lead to others using them for their own desires and agendas and it happens in families, friendships, and far too often in the church. A person's true motivational gift might actually be service, but in using their serving as covering to be acceptable, they are often unable to say no when necessary. Unfortunately, that can lead to being used abusively. The mask also covers their hearts with a false identity and an acceptance coming from what they *do* instead of who they *are created to be*. It's out of our being, out of our hearts, that true service comes and it's from there that God's Spirit can lead us. Jesus reminds us that it's from our innermost being that rivers of living waters flow (John 7:38). Living water comes from the life of God within us that brings a release of life to others as it flows from our willing heart and our unique gifts. It comes from the Spirit-led motivation of our hearts, not from trying to be accepted by others.

When we've lived with a mask for so long, we are no longer in touch with our true self and we've abandoned the life that comes from our hearts. We live from outside of our heart, a life of pretense. Instead of being the person God has created, has always known and loved, we create a person that seems much more acceptable. We sometimes live a life of just survival and duty, trying to meet other's expectations. Unfortunately, we can even pick a career like that and wonder why it feels like drudgery, never bringing us joy.

Sometimes, instead of being "a pleaser," another mask we might choose to hide behind is a mask of "a loser." If we don't try very hard at anything, no one will ever discover we believe we don't measure up and then we don't risk being discovered as a failure. One young man I'll call Kirk, was fearful of getting a job so he always had excuses as to why he couldn't. He seemed to believe his excuses, at least on the surface, but underneath lurked the terror of being found out as a failure. Unfortunately, Kirk was not even conscious of what he was doing. The fear of failure can be birthed out of a buried shame-based lie about ourselves that unknowingly drives our behavior. At one time we might have experienced failure at something we attempted to do, but have remained captive to that buried fear. In that case, bringing the original failure to the light, forgiving ourselves for it as well as any others that were involved and inviting God to heal the memory can bring release. We may have false beliefs about ourselves that have come in through difficult circumstances, beginning sometimes when we were very young, that sabotage our lives without our realizing it. Those lies must be brought to the light in order for us to get out of agreement with them.

A mask can take many forms, but we usually don't question the fact that it might not be the real us. The mask might take the form of a good girl or guy, a pleaser, a yes person, a performer, a macho guy, the smart and capable one, or the opposite, the dumb blonde or airhead. It could be the perfectionist who always excels at everything and is extremely responsible, or the avoider who procrastinates and is irresponsible. As a tough girl or guy, the mask could have a hard exterior and have an opinion on everything, or perhaps the opposite, the passive one, detached and never really present. It might be saccharine sweet and accommodating, or always angry, sarcastic, explosive, and aggressive. It might be the never serious clown who has been the life of the party, or the wallflower who has closed down and hidden themselves behind the potted plants in public gatherings.

The mask can be used to cover our hidden feelings of powerlessness, shame, fear of rejection, abandonment, or any other emotion in order to distance from the terror of the painful past repeating itself. In his book, *Wild at Heart*, John Eldredge writes,

"From the place of our woundedness we construct a false self. We find a few gifts that work for us, and we try to live off them." No matter how much we hide, God has always known our true selves. God knew the real us before we were ever born and He has always loved and accepted us. His heart lovingly desires to bring forth the one He knows so we can fulfill the days ordained for us (Psalm 139). His desire is to unveil the one who makes His heart glad.

The words you use when you talk to and about yourself say a lot about your beliefs regarding your self-worth. Is your self-talk affirming, forgiving, loving, nurturing, or is it laced with put-downs and self-hatred? While at a church gathering, a woman shared with me she's discovering that she's really likeable! Up to now, this woman has been filled with self-hatred. Because of the healing she's currently experiencing, for the first time she's beginning to find herself quite enjoyable. Do you care for yourself in ways that express love? For example, do you care for your body through healthy eating and exercise? Or is it easier to care for other's needs, ignoring your own? Both are needed. Is your home a place you enjoy spending time in and does it reflect your personality or do you want to escape it? Is the time spent alone with just yourself and God fulfilling or do you have to fill your life with busyness or avoidance? When you are alone, do you have to continually fill the space with noise of some type, like TV, radio, or music? Why? It's always amazing to hear people tell me that as they progress in their healing, they are enjoying the quiet spaces more.

It can feel dangerous to be *me* because not everyone will accept me. They didn't accept Jesus and He was perfect. When we believe the *lie* that we must be accepted by everyone, we are setting ourselves up to go back into hiding. That is the reason that, at our core, we must receive God's love and acceptance for us. Jesus gives us substance, people don't. Jesus is our center, people are not. People are fickle, they love you and then can turn around and judge you when you haven't pleased them or met their expectation. Because of that buried awareness, we usually do one of several things. We either desperately try to please them and often *sell our soul* in the process, avoid relationships altogether, or we cover our hearts with self-protection. That false protection will cause us to build a wall inside ourselves so we will not care so much if they hurt us. None of those coverings really work, nor do any of those ways of relating enable us to love others wisely or well, building the honest, healthy relationships we all long for. Some say they don't really care about relationships, but that often comes out of being hurt in the past. We were created from the heart relationship of the Trinity to have relationship. Our hearts are meant to connect with God and be in touch with ourselves so we are able to connect with others on the heart level. The amount of time we desire to spend with others will vary greatly depending on our true personality. Getting to know ourselves will enable us to recognize how much time we need to be alone and how much time is healthy for us to be with others, thereby working with the way God created us rather than against ourselves by only trying to please people.

Sadly, we have often given the power of our lives away to others, or even to society, allowing them to tell us who we are and whether or not we're acceptable. This can drive us to try to prove ourselves worthy of acceptance through things like accomplishments, material possessions, or even through collecting friends. No person or thing can give us that acceptance, only God can. It's not just the adult in us who needs to receive the love of Jesus, it's often the little child within who was originally hurt. It's the wounded child locked inside us who needs to be introduced to Jesus, the lover of the children. Jesus loved them even when they didn't act loveable because He could look past their actions to see their heart's hunger and pain.

When children are hurting they will often shut down or act out with unacceptable behavior. A young child I know was deeply hurting over something a sibling had done that caused a tremendous loss for the whole family. Since the matter didn't directly affect this particular child, his parents were unaware that he was hurting too, so no one was available to help him process his pain. The longer he was left alone with his own hurting heart, the more he began to act out in inappropriate ways even though that wasn't his usual behavior. To his parents, it just seemed like one more thing on their already overflowing plate, so of course he experienced the necessary discipline for his actions. It wasn't until someone asked him if he was hurting too, that the dam of pain broke open, and the reason for his unruly behavior was clear. It's easy to forget that children often experience the same emotions we do, but rarely know what to do with them.

I watched so many parents ignore their children's pain because of being so caught up in their own. Too often we are unable to see our children have broken hearts and painful hurts beneath their actions. Of course, their actions may need to be disciplined, but if a child is acting out in a way that is uncharacteristic for them, after disciplining, do we try to determine what might be going on in their heart? Are they feeling left out, unfairly treated, or misunderstood? Is there a loss of some kind or something going on in the family? Was someone cruel to them? We tend to forget that children feel emotional pain just as we do, even as babies. Just as we longed for someone to know, see, and help us in our struggles when we were growing up, our children have the same longing. Their healing can come quickly when someone is there to help them work through their pain so thirty years later they don't have to try to get their healing in a counselor's office. These events can also become teachable moments for them to learn how to receive Jesus' love and to forgive those who hurt them. Remember though, forgiving others comes after feelings have been acknowledged, not before, otherwise the child is learning wrongly to dismiss his own feelings as unimportant. Feelings are not to be lived in, just acknowledged so they can be released.

God desires us to have unveiled faces that are without masks so we can reflect His glory. "Now the Lord is the Spirit, and where the Spirit of the Lord is there is, freedom. And we, who with unveiled faces all reflect the Lord's glory, are being transformed into His likeness with ever-increasing glory, which comes from the Lord, who is the Spirit." (2 Corinthians 3:17, 18)

"This is love; not that we loved God, but that He loved us and sent His Son as an atoning sacrifice for our sins. Dear friends, since God so loved us, we also ought to love one another." (1 John 4:10,11) The first person we need to learn to love with the love that God has given to us is ourselves. We need to love and receive that little child locked inside even though others might have given us the message that we were unacceptable. Jesus tells us to, "Love your neighbor as yourself" (Matthew 22:39). We can't truly love our neighbor from the heart if we don't love ourselves. Love flows from God's heart to ours, but then we need to receive that love so it can flow out through us to our neighbor.

Questions to Ponder

If I hide myself behind a mask, why?

What does my mask look like?

What do I believe about myself that I feel I must hide?

What kind of a mask might you be wearing without realizing it?

What are some signs that you are not really living from your true heart, but instead from a mask?

What could you do to cooperate with the Spirit in the task of finding the real you?

Assignment

Invite the Holy Spirit to show you when you are fearing man by wearing a mask.

Invite the Spirit to introduce you to yourself, the real self he has always known even before you were ever born (Psalm 139:1,2,13-16 and Ephesians 1:4-6).

Begin to listen to your heart, your desires, your hunger, the things you love to do. Discover the things that bring you life when you do them.

Invite the Spirit to show you why you do some of the things you do, especially the things that do not bring you life.

Begin to thank God daily that He loves you just the way you are. When you are feeling bad about yourself, stop the enemy's words of accusation with, "Thank you God, that you love me right now, even with all my mess. Only You can bring beauty out of ashes."

Scripture

"Fear of man will prove to be a snare..." Proverbs 29:25

5

UNSTUCK FROM
PAINFUL EMOTIONS

Anger, Resentment, Fear and Control

---

*"In your anger do not sin. Do not let the sun go down
while you are still angry, and do not give the devil a
foothold." Ephesians 4:26*

One of the reasons we might be afraid of our emotions is that we really don't understand them. We are often concerned that if we allow ourselves to feel, we'll hurt too much and get stuck in the pain. Unfortunately, for far too many, emotions are almost like a foreign language they never learned. As children, there might not have been anyone to help them understand and process their feelings, so they shut down inside and never learned what their emotions were revealing.

Our emotions are simply the voice of our hearts, telling us what it is feeling at any given time. They are speaking, but what are they telling us? It's like a serious pain in our body. If a certain part of our body needs attention because it is hurting or ill, the pain gives us a message. If we continually ignore it, we will eventually have a larger problem. The more information we gather about the particular pain we're feeling, the easier it becomes to find the right treatment to correct the situation. The same is true with our emotions. How can something be healed unless we know what it is? If we ignore our fear or anxiety for too long without discovering the cause, such as a false belief or a need to control, it might erupt as a panic attack. That, unfortunately, will get our attention! Even then, the usual desire is to simply fix the terror through medication without also finding out what our emotions might be revealing. Medications are fine when needed, but just as with our physical bodies, we also want to get to the root of the problem so real healing can come.

Many families have unspoken rules. The verbal or non-verbal rules may go something like this: "Don't cry," "Don't be sad," "Don't be angry," "Don't show anyone your feelings," "Just smile," "Be happy," or something else along those lines. As you can see, we are often programmed to hide our feelings under a mask. One person I knew always greeted others with, "Happy, happy, happy!" We so desire to live "happily ever after!" Another woman once told me she was taught from early childhood to always smile and be nice, but never let anyone know how she really felt.

Let's see if we can demystify our emotions. There are certain processes that are true whether they are playing out in our spirits, in our souls (in the emotional part of our soul) or in our bodies. Healing is one of these processes so the same steps required to care for our bodies are necessary in the other areas as well. When there are problems in our natural bodies, a diagnosis can be helpful to get us to the real issue instead of just treating the symptoms. Nurturing is similar in that care is required. Just as we nurture our bodies by feeding and taking care of them, the same attention is needed for our spirits and emotions to remain healthy.

The same people who tended to the sickness in our physical bodies when we were growing up, often ignored our emotional needs, struggles, and pain. This is not to blame our parents because they couldn't give to us what they didn't have for themselves. Sadly, many of our parents never had the opportunity to heal from their own emotional pain. In spite of that, we must now face what was never acknowledged to begin with and left buried deep within. Then, as those emotions are allowed to surface, we can be healed and move toward the heart forgiveness of those who failed us, not just excuse or forgive them from our head alone.

As Christians, we rightly look to God to meet our *spiritual hunger*, which is very necessary and good. However, what we sometimes don't realize is that if we still have buried *emotional hunger*, it will drive us in directions that are not always good in order to meet that need. An example of this would be when we are outside of a spiritual environment and we're driven to do the very things we don't want to do. How many promises are made to God in church that cannot be maintained during the week? As usual, there can be more than one reason for that. However, one that we're sometimes not aware of is that if our heart hunger has been buried, it can leak out in various ways, driving us from within and displaying itself in our actions. One way it played out in my life years ago was, whenever I felt alone for any reason, my old childhood loneliness would surface and I would be driven to make connection with someone. It wasn't just a choice to pick up the phone; I was compelled to contact someone to ease the emptiness I felt. Jesus tells us that it's from the heart that our actions come. If we are feeling driven, then what is that telling us about our heart? Often it's simply revealing there is an unhealed area of hunger from the past that is driving us.

Our hunger is to be felt and embraced because it is meant to lead us to God on an emotionally deep heart level. Emotional intimacy with God fills the emptiness within us. What if it's the three-year old within us who is feeling emotionally starved? What if we never received nurturing as a child? Many people share with me that no one ever told them they were loved, valued, accepted and enjoyed. Others' parents told them over and over that they were loved, but as children, a heart connection with their own parents was never experienced, so it all felt empty. Their parents provided many things and they were never in want in the physical realm, but all the while their hearts were starving. A scenario like that can make us feel guilty for even desiring more and cause us to hide the hunger that then comes out in inappropriate ways.

Many things can be used to fill our empty hearts, one of

which can be to *use* people instead of truly loving them. When we do that, we develop co-dependent relationships, which are *use* relationships and not healthy ones. Even in marriage, sex can be *use* instead of love. We can *use* work for more than provision and, instead, be driven to success and money to fill our insecurity and emptiness. Isaiah 44:12-20 gives us an interesting picture of how our work is used to get food and warmth, which is good, but then how part of it can also be used as an idol that we worship. Unfortunately, we can use our work to hide ourselves in or to prove ourselves acceptable to others. An idol isn't just an image made out of wood or stone, it can be anything we are putting our trust in above God or instead of Him. Sometimes, even ministry and helping others is used to fill the ache within, an ache we are no longer attuned to. We might use food or drink, toys, computer games, drugs, the Internet or anything else that is soul numbing. Sadly, many times life is lived vicariously through TV, movies, or novels. We cry for others, but never for ourselves and for that little child within who has been lost and left starving.

"Give me an undivided heart" (Psalm 86:11). Will we allow the Spirit who searches all things, to show us our buried emotional hunger? Will we allow ourselves to connect with the hunger of that little child who has been lost within us? Doing so enables Jesus to meet us in that hunger to begin the process of filling the emptiness with his love.

How old is that child? How long has the soul hunger been there? Those are questions to ask the Spirit of God. It takes our joining with Him in the nurturing of our little one for the empty cup to be filled, thus beginning the re-growth and integration process. Remember, Jesus is outside of time and can go back into our past as well as ahead into our future to set us free. He needs us to join with Him on behalf of that lost, little child within us. Let us never forget that He came "to seek and to save what was lost" (Luke 10:10). We also need to remember what Jesus reveals is an important part of His mission: He came to bind up the broken-hearted. How do we join with Him in feeding that little child?

We can begin by listening to him or her. What is the emotional hunger they are still carrying? What did they desire that was left unacknowledged? Sometimes it takes time and willingness to allow the Spirit to reintroduce us to that little one who has been lost for so long.

Emotions need not be fearful, although at times they can be painful. That emotional pain can be revealing just as our physical pain reveals that something within needs healing. Ask yourself, "What am I feeling?" Our emotions need to be felt and acknowledged as our own. They are our emotions and they are speaking to us. So what are they saying? Invite God to show you. Look at the list of emotions in chapter nine. Ask, "When did I feel that emotion before?" "How old was I when I did?" Once we listen, we can begin the process of dealing with them appropriately. Maybe they're telling us we're angry. Ask the Spirit of God to help you know why you feel angry. What just happened? Were you treated unfairly, rejected, overlooked, or shamed? Is that how you felt in the past? Did someone (possibly even God) thwart something you were trying to control? Emotions cannot be fully released until they are first owned.

Anger

Maybe you are angry, but you don't even know it. A test I took over 30 years ago said 95% of my anger was buried, yet I had no idea it was even there! Perhaps there was abuse or injustice in your life as there was in mine, but you weren't *allowed* to be angry, so anger was not acknowledged in your house. Perhaps the opposite is true. One parent raged at the drop of a hat, so you vowed never to be like them! Because I was unaware of the anger I carried, I never acknowledged it so it could be worked through. As a result, my anger came out as depression with occasional bouts of rage. Some people display anger as aggression, but for others it goes inward toward themselves as depression. An emotion must be felt in order to work it through; otherwise it just goes underground or can come out in an explosion. It's amazing how my depressive personality changed after I finally faced my anger! Sometimes a person might appear to have a very calm personality, but inside, offenses are building. My mother was like that, she was extremely sweet, but about every six months the volcano would erupt. That can be extremely damaging to all who get the fallout because you usually never see it coming. When we learn how to face our anger, working it through in each situation, those volcanic explosions begin to be a thing of the past. We no longer store our anger up inside.

Anger is energy. Ask, "How can I release this energy in a healthy way?" Go to the gym? Run? Work in the garden? Recently my husband went out to wash the car, but what was unusual was that he never does that. It turns out that he was dealing with anger about something, so that was a healthy way of working out the energy that was building inside. However, while releasing it, try to put words to the anger. "I feel angry because…" For me, the best way to release my anger is to write, to journal. Instead of just generally writing out my feelings, I write letters to God and share with Him all my emotions, the good, the bad, and the ugly. God knows about it anyway, and since He knows me at the deepest level of my heart, He is never shocked. When writing, don't write from your head, but write from deep within. Write out your feelings, not just the facts.

Another way is to write a letter to the one you're angry with; a letter that is never going to be sent or seen. The letter is a way to give a voice to your feelings and is for your eyes alone. Then, when you have owned and released the feelings, work toward forgiving that person and destroy the letter. At that point, if it is still necessary to speak to the other about it, your feelings will have been diffused, you will be calmer and, as a result, it is likely the person will not react as defensively. We are usually able to communicate with others much more effectively after writing out our feelings and releasing them. An important thing is to begin changing our communication to, "I feel…" instead of, "You always…" which only makes the other party defensive. "In your anger, do not sin" (Ephesians 4:26). It never says not to be angry, but just don't act it out or bury it within. Since we have to do something with the anger in order not to sin, the above suggestions can be a helpful way of dealing with it. It's important, though, to be careful we don't replay the situation over and over again in our mind or with others. Once we have acknowledged we're angry and written out why, it's time for it to be released it so we can get in touch with the feelings beneath it.

Anger can be a covering emotion, similar to a lid on a box. After removing the lid of anger, what emotions are still in the box? You might find disappointed expectations, desires, longings or even a loss of some kind. Perhaps you are sad and grieving over your picture of the way you thought things would turn out. Maybe you felt betrayed, rejected, dismissed, disregarded or overlooked by someone you cared about. There could be feelings of powerlessness, embarrassment, or feeling exposed and shamed before the eyes of others. There might even be envy or jealousy. I sometimes used to feel jealousy around a certain friend. Because jealousy seemed like such an ugly emotion I tried to bury it, however, it wasn't until I owned my jealousy that release came. From that time on, I no longer had a struggle with it and could enjoy her blessings.

People who are afraid to speak up can feel very powerless in certain situations so their immediate reaction is often anger. One woman would get very angry inside at her husband's frequent explosions that were mostly directed at her. Much earlier, she had lost her voice with him and became afraid to speak up, so each time it happened, she felt trapped with feelings of helplessness and hopelessness. His verbal attack was abusive, but it took a while for her to see that and begin to allow her anger to be worked through to the courage to draw a line in the sand with him. As she finally did, each time it happened she used the same reply that it was no longer acceptable for him to speak to her that way and, if he continued, she would go to another room, being ready to leave the house if necessary. It took time, but he began to develop a new respect for her with only an occasional slip up which she was then able to handle as soon as it happened. Anger, when worked through, can become courage, much like the courage Jesus had when he stood up to the religious leaders and cleaned the temple after they had made it a den of robbers (Mark 11:15-17).

Since anger feels powerful and preferable to feeling helpless, we will frequently unknowingly choose it. However, if we don't allow ourselves to feel the powerlessness under the anger, we will remain stuck. It is in our powerlessness that Christ's strength is made perfect (2 Corinthians 12:9,10). When we own our feelings of powerlessness, it can enable us to begin to draw on Christ's strength while experiencing our weakness and not be shamed by our own inadequacies. Jesus was crucified in weakness (powerlessness), yet He lived by God's power (2 Corinthians 13:4). If He lived by God's power, why would we think we could do things on our own? He reminds us that "apart from me you can do nothing" (John 15:5). We have been created to be dependent on God and His power, but the lie tells us that we should be strong enough to never be so helpless. Those verses remind us of the exchange process He makes with us. When we face our feelings of weakness, powerlessness, or helplessness, we can exchange them for the strength and power of Jesus. Anger is difficult to let go of, but as God continually reminds me, "Your anger does not work my purposes in your life."

Resentment

Anger that has not been faced often remains hidden deep inside as resentment. One way we can get a clue as to whether we might be holding resentment toward someone is by thinking of the person who hurt us and then honestly answering questions like, "Does my heart feel warm toward that person?" If not, "Do I feel anger or even *nothing at all* when I think of them?" "Might I have closed my heart toward them?" "If I were to be brutally transparent with myself, do I secretly wish for them to pay?" "Would I silently like revenge?" In his book, *The Search for Significance*, Robert S. McGee points out four common lies we often believe as truth. The third lie mentioned is, "Those who fail are unworthy of love and deserve to be punished." Ask God to show you if you have believed that lie? When first reading the book, I didn't relate to that false belief at all, but not long after God showed me that lie was hiding deep inside my heart and operated in many ways, hurting others as well as myself.

Un-faced resentment can live within us for many years, even a lifetime. It poisons us from within. It's also toxic to others because it leaks out in comments or an attitude and builds a wall around our hearts. Sadly, it can also become a "root of bitterness that grows up to cause trouble and defile many" (Hebrews 12:15). Resentment can in some cases also leak into our bodies and contribute toward things like arthritis, skin disorders, head and neck aches, as well as various other problems.

Fear and Control

Many are driven by fear. I was for many years. Fear breeds control and control often comes from the desperate need to hold the world together, *our* world. In childhood, our lives might have felt unsafe because there was no one there to keep us feeling safe and secure. This can happen from living with uncertainty in an alcoholic family or in a family with a single parent who is just overwhelmed by trying to make life work. It can also happen when there is trauma in childhood, like abuse of any kind. It can happen from having wounded parents who never faced their own insecurities and fears. When any of those situations are experienced as children, we can learn to become hyper-vigilant and on high alert at all times trying to keep our life safe, but underneath, we are fearful of being caught by surprise. Children are meant to be at rest with others more capable than they are protecting and caring for their needs. When that doesn't happen, they have to pretend to be adults, even while they are children. Like myself, I know so many others who lost the joy of childhood very early on because of feeling like they had to be the adult and hold their family together when of course they couldn't even begin to know how. Out of my feeling so unsafe at four or five years old, I can remember checking all the doors before I could sleep each night. That's the job of a parent, not a small child. I couldn't control the big things, but that was one thing I could do to keep my world feeling a little safer.

In our present adult relationships, when healing from childhood hurts has not taken place, we can sometimes have strong emotions of fear playing out. One that we might experience is the fear of being abandoned and left all alone. The fear of being left alone and abandoned can cause a person to cling and hold on too tightly; smothering the one they care about. At the same time, they might be trying to *pull* something from the other to fill their ever-present childhood neediness. This can cause the other person to want to flee. It triggers *the other's* fear of being consumed or smothered and can cause them to want to distance from the very one they care about. Although it might not cause an actual fleeing, it can come in the form of emotional distancing. Unfortunately, the more one pulls away, the more the other tries to cling and hold on! Sadly, that fear of abandonment/smother cycle can play over and over with neither recognizing what is really going on and can sometimes switch back and forth between the two parties becoming almost like a dance.

So often in marriage one is dominant while the other is passive and almost absent. Yes, opposites attract which is a good thing, but when one partner loses themselves, their voice, and their personality for the sake of the other, that is not good. Where is their heart? What happened to it? Did they give it up it in order to keep the relationship intact? As a favorite author of mine, Dan Allender, writes in his powerful book, *The Wounded Heart*, "To love is to be more committed to the other than we are to the relationship, to be more concerned about his walk with God than the comfort or benefits of his walk with us." Often we just want to keep our relationship intact, so we sell our soul to do so. It is often done to keep a peace that is not really peace at all. Jesus said He didn't "come to bring peace, but a sword" (Matthew 10:34-39). A sword is sometimes necessary to cut through the false systems that have been built to make life work the way we think we need it to.

The fear of rejection is similar to the fear of abandonment, but often has a little different flavor. One of the things that can cause rejection to feel so painful is the shame we experience when we feel rejected. Because the deep hurt of rejection often has to do with feeling exposed before others' eyes as not being worthy of acceptance and enjoyment, we often experience the pain of believing we are being rejected because we are deficient. Of course, that's a lie. We are a "pearl of great price" that Jesus sold all to buy back (Matthew 13:45,46). However, until we face the wound of rejection that is still lodging within us from past situations, we are usually not able to hold onto that truth in our hearts. We might hear it, agree with it in our heads, but the truth does not remain until the lie of rejection we have believed has been acknowledged and released. When we do that, Jesus is able to make an exchange with us there because He has also had the experience of being "despised and rejected of men" (Isaiah 53:2,3). The good news is that Jesus is able to connect with us in our terrible pain of rejection so we can exchange it for His true acceptance and love.

"I have chosen you and not rejected you. So do not fear, for I am with you; do not be dismayed, for I am your God. I will strengthen you and help you; I will uphold you with my righteous right hand." (Isaiah 41:9b,10)

For so many years, I lived with anxiety within, waiting for the other shoe to drop. I was unable to relax and always had to be on high alert so when that shoe dropped, I wouldn't be caught off guard. Anxiety is diffused fear, many times coming from fearing the loss of control, but it isn't always felt as fear and instead it could be experienced as dread and apprehension. Sometimes I felt like there was an out-of-control motor racing in my chest with no way to turn it off. Anxiety doesn't let us rest so even when it should be a relaxing, fun time, we remain on guard. We may live with those feelings for most of our lives, not realizing it's not how we're created to live. It almost seems normal, especially when we've grown up with turmoil, but of course it's not since we're meant to live in the peace and rest Jesus died to give us. Because we're so wonderfully woven together in spirit, soul, and body, anxiety not only affects our mind and heart, but our body as well. When a motor would race in my chest, I found that taking a number of deep breaths and holding them for 5 seconds or so would ease the tension in my chest. That would take my attention off my body so I could look at the fear or the loss of control that was causing my anxiety. "You will keep in perfect peace him whose mind is steadfast, because he trusts in you" (Isaiah 26:3).

Living with un-faced anxiety and fear can lead to the need for control. It can drive us to attempt to control other people, ourselves, situations and sometimes even God. It's a way to try to create life as we desire it to be in order to feel safe. In other words, we are running our own world and not allowing God to do it because we are afraid on the deepest level of our hearts to really trust Him. This can happen when we have felt betrayed by a parent or other authority figure earlier in our lives. Far too many people I've known had their ability to trust destroyed from the abuse they suffered as children. The ones that were meant to protect and keep them emotionally, physically or sexually safe abandoned and betrayed them. When we've experienced any major betrayal like that, it can affect our ability to trust on a deep heart level.

Trust gets betrayed in various ways in our relationships, but two of the greatest ways are through abuse of any kind, especially sexual, and through infidelity in marriage. Once trust has been broken and deeply betrayed, we often have a long and difficult time getting it back. Jesus *entrusted* Himself to no man because He knew what was in a man (John 2:24,25). Our hearts can only truly be *entrusted* to God Himself because only He can be fully trusted to care for them. He is then able to begin to teach us discernment and wisdom in relationships. Without this discernment, many times we will either try to cover our hearts with self-protection, which prevents love, or have a false, foolish trust in man often combined with the magical thinking that we will never be hurt. We all wound each other even when we desire not to because hurt people hurt each other. However, that does not make light of it or give excuse to our continual wounding of one another. Sadly, another generation will be affected if we do not deal with our hurts.

In my life, my father was driven by fear and insecurity and without realizing it he passed it on to me. Because of this, as a very young child, I felt his insecurity and began the impossible task of holding life together. Since a child is to be cared for, they haven't been created to hold their world together and of course aren't equipped to do so. After becoming a parent myself, because I hadn't yet faced that fear, I sadly passed much of it on to my own children. Seeing that brought great sadness and was a part of what finally motivated me to face myself. The circumstances God allowed to come into my life that were too big for me to hold together finally got my attention. Bit by bit He pried my fingers loose of trying to control. Because of the desperation I felt as my world slowly fell apart in a number of directions at once, I had to begin to let go because nothing seemed to work any longer. The process took well over a year and during it I felt battered on every side.

What I discovered though, is that He is enough, and "He is before all things, and in Him all things hold together" (Colossians 1:17). We are also reminded that He "sustains all things by His powerful word" (Hebrews 1:3). I believe God's desire is that we willingly let go without having to be backed into a corner like I was. The pressure He allowed me to experience eventually caused me to surrender my will to Him, which was His desire all along. Not having dealt with my anxiety and control earlier in life, caused a lot of unnecessary pain for my family. Sadly, as my father did before me, I caused that spirit of fear to be passed on to another generation.

Trusting God with our minds might not be so difficult, but it's our hearts that are afraid to risk again once we've been deeply hurt. If we have been betrayed by an authority figure of any kind, such as a parent, we can tend to project that onto how we view and are able to trust God. We can then become fearful to really let go of our control on the deepest level of the heart. We will often attempt to orchestrate our own life and the lives of others according to our rules, because it feels safer that way. This can also cause us to feel guilty since we know we're supposed to be trusting God to do that, resting in Him. Trust in God is necessary if we are to come through our wounded emotions to a place of peace and be able to enjoy healthy relationships. However, when we've experienced betrayal God knows how our trust was robbed. His desire is not to condemn, but to meet us in our pain and walk us through to healing and rest. However, He needs us to cooperate with Him so our pain can finally be exchanged for His healing. "Be still, and know that I am God" (Psalm 46:10).

Our fear-driven control can sometimes manifest in the form of manipulation, intimidation, or domination. Even when we are good at recognizing one form of control such as manipulation, because perhaps we had a parent who operated that way, we might miss it when it comes in the form of intimidation or domination. I had clearly recognized control in several forms, but a spirit of intimidation still trapped me for several years before I cried out to God to show me what was wrong. I had been given the opportunity to lead a women's ministry, but strangely was unable to actually do it and didn't know why. Instead, I felt paralyzed. It wasn't until the Lord showed me the intimidation that was operating around me and had stolen my voice that I saw things clearly. Even though I had permission to minister, I was unable to on a corporate level because I was under a spirit of intimidation that was operating without my even realizing it.

If you struggle with control, ask the Lord to show you what fear might be driving it. When struggling with fear or anxiety, I encourage you to ask the question, "What am I really afraid of?" Put words to your fear to get it into the light. "I am afraid because…" There might be several layers to your fears and by facing the first one a way is made to go deeper. Jesus wants to put the axe to the root of it and not just cover it over with a band-aid. Under the fear is usually a false belief, so the next question is, "What do I believe on a deep level of my heart that is causing me to fear?" Remember, it is the Spirit who searches out the deep things within us, so invite Him to help you. Be patient to wait since these things often surface when we relax. It usually happens to me while driving down the road or in doing some mindless task, but rarely when I am pressing for it. So just be willing to invite the Spirit to show you when He finds you are ready.

As we begin to face our fears, the next step is to move toward surrendering them to God. In order to do that, we will probably have to wrestle with the question, "God, is your heart toward me really *good*?" If we do not believe on a deep heart level that God's heart is *good toward us*, we will likely be unable to surrender our specific fears to Him. We have to understand that although His heart toward us is good, He won't always do things the way we demand. Letting go of those demands moves us toward trusting Him. The sign that our heart has been surrendered to Him and His ways, even when we don't understand them, is peace. We might believe we've surrendered because we said it with our mouth, but if we're not resting in peace the surrender has not yet gotten to our heart.

Questions to Ask God

"God, please show me if there is any anger that has been buried within me." Signs of buried anger might be depression, judgments, or unexpected explosions.

"God, how might I be trying to hold my world together? If I am, what do I believe will happen if I don't?"

"Do I struggle with control? If so, what form does it come in – intimidation, domination, manipulation or in some other way?"

Anytime you might be feeling anxious, ask: "God is there something I am trying to control?"

"I am afraid of_____."

"I am afraid because_____."

"God, is there a false belief or lie under that fear? Please reveal it to me."

Assignment

Write a letter to God about your anger, telling Him everything you are feeling.

Write a letter to anyone you still have anger toward (a letter that will never be shared with them) and put words to your feelings.

After expressing your emotions, begin the process of releasing your judgment to God and moving toward them with heart forgiveness even if it's not deserved. You might begin by earnestly praying blessings upon them. Forgiveness sets you free!

Scriptures

"For my thoughts are not your thoughts, neither are your ways my ways, declares the Lord. As the heavens are higher than the earth, so are my ways higher than your ways, and my thoughts than your thoughts." Isaiah 55:8,9

"God is our refuge and strength, an ever-present help in trouble. Therefore we will not fear, though the earth give way and the mountains fall into the heart of the sea, though its waters roar and foam and the mountains quake with their surging. There is a river whose streams make glad the city of God, the holy place where God dwells. God is within her, she will not fall; God will help her at the break of day." Psalm 46:1-5

"Cease striving, and know that I am God." Psalm 46:10 NAS

"But I trust in you, O Lord; I say, 'You are my God', my times are in your hands..." Psalm 31:14,15

6
SEPARATING REAL FROM FALSE

Healthy and Unhealthy Guilt,
Shame, Responsibility

"Surely you desire truth in the inner parts; you teach me
wisdom in the inmost place." Psalm 51:6

Healthy guilt is a warning from God through our conscience that we have sinned. It keeps us humble by causing us to remain aware that we're not God and certainly not perfect. The book of Romans confirms this by reminding us that we have all sinned and come short of God's glory (Romans 3:23). However, the wonder of the cross proclaims that God understands our nature so forgiveness is available if we will own our sin and humbly go to Jesus to ask for it. Unfortunately, we will at times find a person with an over-developed conscience because of unhealed wounds that causes them to operate out of a false sense of guilt. There are those who live each day with a dull sense of dread and guilt hanging over them, but never realize their guilt is false. Too often they just experience condemnation from the guilty feelings instead of using them as an opportunity to ask God if they are coming from any real guilt of their own. God never brings condemnation, that's the enemy's mode of operation. "Therefore, there is now no condemnation for those who are in Christ Jesus" (Romans 8:1). Instead, God gently convicts by pricking our conscience.

Because there are two types of guilt, just as there are two types of shame, it becomes important to recognize how they differ. For

example, a mother of one person I know continually puts her disappointed expectations on her daughter in the form of guilt. If the
daughter doesn't do what the mother wants, she "guilts" her into
obedience. In that case, the guilt is the mother's not the daughter's,
but the daughter is just now learning to recognize that and come
out from under the burden. If you have lived under false guilt for
a very long time, it might be necessary to run a guilt-producing
situation by someone who is emotionally healthy before you deal
with it. A clue as to whether or not the guilt might be false can also
be recognized in how it makes you feel. If the guilt is coming from
something we've done in opposition to the scriptures and will of
God or purposely left undone, our guilt is real and something we
need to take ownership for. However, the good news is we then
have the opportunity to bring that to the cross, receive forgiveness,
and make restitution wherever necessary. For the forgiveness to
be complete, however, it must be received as well as asked for. If
Jesus has forgiven us, who are we to say, "That's not sufficient,"
and continue to pay for something He gave His life for?

Sometimes there are other stumbling blocks that keep us from
resting in the forgiveness Jesus paid for. For example, we might
be able to own our sin and feel genuinely repentant, but then the
unworthiness we feel, which is really shame, prevents us from
accepting the forgiveness we asked for. The reality is that we *are*
within ourselves unworthy, but that's the beauty of Jesus' sacrifice
for us. He takes our unworthiness upon Himself and exchanges it
for His acceptance based on His worth, not on ours. "God made
Him who had no sin to be sin for us, so that in Him we might
become the righteousness of God" (2 Corinthians 5:21).

Another thing that might be preventing our enjoyment of
forgiveness is the real guilt from something in the past we are
still trying to bury. By inviting the Spirit to search our hearts,
we're giving Him permission to reveal that past event and to
bring it to our consciousness. In facing it honestly, we are freed to
finally bring it to the cross for forgiveness, cleansing, and healing.
"Blessed is he whose transgressions are forgiven, whose sins are

covered… When I kept silent, my bones wasted away through my groaning all day long" (Psalm 32:1&3). God is a God of light and when we have things of darkness buried inside us that we still feel guilty over, it is like a poison within us. We might have tried to push the feeling away, but since the guilt is darkness, we can still be affected by it, too often even in our bodies. However, the good news is that as soon as "we confess our sins, he is faithful and just and will forgive us our sins and purify us from all unrighteousness" (1 John 1:9).

False Guilt

Unfortunately, false guilt cannot just be forgiven like that because it's not ours to own. How does false guilt get a hold on our lives? One way would be that we might have been disciplined through guilt and shame and made to feel guilty as children. In that case, it's not our guilt, but the guilt of the one who disciplined us wrongly. Some parents use guilt to keep their children in line, feeling they won't stray if their conscience is super-sensitized. When those children become adults, they will often feel guilty over most everything and are sometimes unable to enjoy life in a healthy way. They might live a guarded, carefully boxed-in life, being prone to legalism instead of freedom in Jesus. Depending on personality, sometimes that upbringing causes the opposite to happen which paves the road to rebellion.

Without realizing it, other parents have passed down their own guilty feelings to their children because they never dealt with the guilt in themselves. I've seen examples of this with parents projecting onto their children all sorts of behaviors that were not even in the child's heart to do, but instead came out of their parent's past. As a parent myself there were times when, out of fear, I accused my son of behaviors that were from my dysfunctional past and not even in his heart to do. I can now certainly understand the resentment it created and how I wish, as so many parents do, that I could have a do-over, but only God can restore the past.

Because of the legalism false guilt can produce in us, we might try harder and harder to do things right to release the guilty feelings. Of course, that never works because it is not the way Jesus paid for. He offers us a gift of grace that none of us deserve. In order to receive that grace, humility is needed, not self-righteousness. For those held captive under false guilt, grace can be something that is difficult to receive for ourselves, as well as give to others. The wonderful thing is, the more we are able to receive it for ourselves, the more we can gracefully extend it to others.

False guilt cannot be forgiven; it must be recognized and gotten out of agreement with because it's not our guilt. Some who struggle with it have a false belief or lie lodged deep within that tells them their heart is bad. God gave us a new heart and a new spirit when we received Jesus and removed that old heart of stone (Ezekiel 36:26). The truth is, our new heart is good because it comes from God. As we accept that, our responsibility is to grow in our walk with Him and cooperate with His Spirit so the fruit of his love is able to come through us more and more.

False or Illegitimate Shame

Shame is similar to guilt; however, illegitimate or false shame often connects to a core belief that is really a lie buried deep within us. If you are burdened by the emotions of unworthiness, feeling like you never measure up, are never fully acceptable, or struggle with the fear of inadequacy or fear of failure, you might have a core, illegitimate, false-shame belief that needs to be recognized and brought to the light. Once we have faced this as the lie it is, we can begin the process of getting out of agreement with it. When the shame we feel does not tie into something we have legitimately done or neglected to do, it is false or illegitimate shame and not ours, although we have carried it as our own. Whose shame is it? Who are we carrying that shame for? An example would be abuse. The person who has experienced abuse usually feels deep shame even though the shame was not theirs. It was the shame of the one who abused them. To come out from under the lie of the shame, it is necessary to recognize that and no longer emotionally carry it for the abuser. If a child has been abused, it is never the child's fault. Adults are meant to care for and protect children, not harm, use, and abuse them.

As with guilt, we can be shamed as children through poor discipline, with words, an attitude, or even a look and those ways of shaming others can unfortunately be passed down from generation to generation. In my time of growing up, it was common for discipline not to be clean. Wagging an index finger with disdain on their face, a common rebuke was, "Shame on you!" Afterward, you were often emotionally banished and cut off from family fellowship for a time. That not only caused shame, but also feelings of rejection and abandonment because you never knew when or if you would be included again. I so enjoy watching parents today who discipline their children cleanly by taking them into another room so as not to shame them before others' eyes, dealing with the issue at hand, giving consequences when needed, but afterward hugging them to assure them they are still loved and accepted. Shame can also be absorbed through the atmosphere of a home when the parents are shame-based themselves. It seems as though just like a virus, it can be caught.

Because my father was wounded and shame-based himself, it seems the only love he felt free to give was through teasing and shame. Many times when my dad would get close to uncomfortable emotions, he would deflect by using teasing, some of which was fairly cruel. I know now, after a lot of healing, that because of his fear of vulnerability, it was a safe way for him to show love. Unfortunately, that didn't communicate love to me as a child. Instead, it only contributed to my shame belief that I was unacceptable and not worth loving, seeing, knowing, or enjoying.

Shame can also come in through humiliating experiences in childhood, such as when we were embarrassed in front of our peers, through teachers, or other authority figures. It might have come through other children when we were continually mocked, laughed at, and excluded while we were simply longing to be enjoyed and included. I was never good at sports so I remember the agony in gym class when I would be the last one chosen for a team. That only added to the wound of rejection I lived with and the shame I felt over my inadequacy.

One of the most damaging causes of viewing ourselves with shame can come from abuse of any kind, especially sexual abuse, because that affects how we view ourselves in our sexuality as men and women. Abuse can cause our understanding of love, both toward ourselves and others, to be damaged and twisted as well. It can cause someone to either struggle with promiscuity or be shut down sexually in marriage. Sadly, it causes relational problems throughout our lives until it is dealt with, as well as causing us difficulty in being able to fully trust God. Many times, those who have experienced abuse will begin to hate even their God-given longings to ever be wanted and enjoyed. I did, feeling that if I had never desired in the first place, I wouldn't have hurt so much. When we've experienced abuse of any kind, we might have developed beliefs about ourselves that were not true, but remained deeply hidden in our hearts until finally brought to the light for healing. Those false beliefs or lies are usually buried so deeply within us, that it takes the help of the Spirit of God to surface them. Once faced, we must challenge the truth of them, finally seeing them as the lies they are. When in the light, our false beliefs can be replaced with the truth of God's word, enabling us to begin to receive His love and acceptance of us. For anyone desiring to heal from the horrors of sexual abuse, I highly recommend Dr. Dan Allender's liberating book and workbook entitled, *The Wounded Heart*.

False or illegitimate shame attacks the person. For example, false shame is an "I" belief as opposed to "I have done…" reality. The scripture reminds us that we have all sinned and come short of the glory of God; therefore, we have all done things that need forgiveness (Romans 3:23,24). When we acknowledge our sin and ask for forgiveness, we are forgiven because of Jesus' sacrifice and our acceptance of His sacrifice so we can feel clean. However, if we have a false "I" belief, the lie we've believed might sound something like this: "I am a failure," "I'm not enough," "I don't measure up," "I am a mistake." In my case the lie was, "I'm a throwaway, like a piece of garbage."

When we're living with that "I" message or illegitimate shame belief deep within us, we have to recognize it as the lie it is in order to be free. As long as a lie remains hidden and we've not yet gotten out of agreement with it in order to be healed, we will live our daily lives out of that belief. Sadly, it will drive us and affect every part of our lives, often sabotaging our relationships and hurting others. It will cause us to interpret and perceive our interactions and circumstances falsely by reading into other's words and actions things that were not intended. Unfortunately, it can destroy the true relationships our hearts were made for. God is a God of light, not darkness (1 John 1:5, Ephesians 5:8). Lies are darkness. When the lies we have believed as truth are brought to the light, we can begin to get out of agreement with them so that healing can finally begin to come.

God is a God of truth and desires "truth in our innermost being" (Psalm 51:6). It's not enough to have truth in our heads alone. When our shame lie is finally faced and brought to the light, we can begin to replace it with the truth of God's word and, for the first time, the truth begins to touch a deeper place within us. You cannot put truth on top of a lie and expect it to remain. The lie must first be faced and gotten out of agreement with. Have you ever wondered why you can receive a genuine compliment, but it doesn't reach the deepest places within you? Oh, it's nice and you might appreciate it for the moment, but it doesn't really warm your heart. Perhaps the opposite happens, and you pridefully grab hold of the compliment, using it to puff yourself up in a way you know is not good. The Bible reminds us to "...not to think of yourself more highly than you ought, but rather think of yourself with sober judgment..." (Romans 12:3). Shame can cause us to either want to blend into the woodwork and not be seen at all, or the opposite, puff ourselves up, trying to be seen by everybody.

Pride

Pride is the opposite side of the shame coin. Many times we feel guilty for experiencing pride yet not realize that our pride is often driven by our lies of shame. For example, why do we often want to prove ourselves to be more than others, looking or performing better than someone else?

Is that what might be driving extreme competition? Desiring to prove ourselves can come from an expression of pride that is being driven by shame. It can originate in a core-shame belief that we really are less than others and that we don't measure up. We can keep that false belief so buried within that it's hidden even from ourselves and we don't realize our lie is driving us into pride. Sadly, others usually see it before we do. I'm sure others saw the systems I used to prove myself long before I did. The need I lived with for approval from authority figures was driven by the shame belief that I was a throw-away; after all, my own parents never seemed to care.

God promises grace to the humble, but there is a false humility that many of us with shame beliefs have struggled with, sometimes without realizing it. When we are truly humble, we will have an honest, accurate estimation of ourselves, seeing both our strengths and weaknesses without illusion, and not have to either hide or prove ourselves. We begin to know who we are, but at the same time we are fully aware of what Jesus reminds us that without Him we can't do anything (John 15:5), so it doesn't lead to pride.

Before the fall happened, Adam and Eve were "both naked, and they felt no shame" (Genesis 2:25). After the fall, the enemy who was driven by his own pride, the pride that got him thrown out of heaven (Isaiah 14:12-15), lured Adam and Even to become their own gods and no longer depend on the God who created them. "For God knows that when you eat of it your eyes will be opened, and you will be like God knowing good and evil" (Genesis

3:5). What was the first thing that happened when their eyes were opened? "Then the eyes of both of them were opened, and they realized they were naked; so they sewed fig leaves together and made coverings for themselves" (Genesis 3:7). Shame entered the picture. From that point, they tried to hide their shame by covering themselves with fig leaves. We still use fig leaves today, things like performance, success, perfectionism, and a host of other things including blame, to hide the shame of being found out that we're not enough. The truth is we're not enough because we're not meant to be. It's only with Christ living in us that we are once again enough! He completes and restores us.

Glory

As our identity becomes increasingly based in Him, instead of trying to prove ourselves, we begin to see that because of Jesus we have worth. We can finally begin the process of learning to live from the truth that we've been fought for, paid for by his blood, and that He has put His very life in us to reflect Jesus to a hurting world. Realizing that on the heart level allows the life of Jesus to flow into our hearts and then out through us in our own unique way to others. When we begin to do that, we reflect His glory, not ours. Glory is what man was covered with before the fall, coming from the breath of God and breathed into man. That glory was lost and replaced by shame, as we see in Genesis chapter three. (Psalm 4:2) "How long, O men, will you turn my glory into shame?"

Now for any of us who have received Jesus into our lives, His life is once again breathed into us, replacing our core shame with His glory. That is not meant just to be a Bible truth, but something we live from daily. This is a mystery, "Christ in us the hope of glory" (Colossians 1:27). When we are finally able to grasp the reality of this mystery, recognize and release our core-shame beliefs, it is life changing, releasing in us a new understanding and purpose for living. "For in Him we live and move and have our being" (Acts 17:28). It also paves the way for a new identity that comes from God Himself (Isaiah 62:2-4). Instead of an identity born in the shame lie, we begin to learn who we are in Christ and who He is in us.

Even though my core shame beliefs were hidden from me for 50 years, I still lived out of them everyday until they were recognized. Every shame belief that's buried has words attached. My words were based on what life had communicated to me, beginning at a very young age. As mentioned above, my particular words were, "You are a throwaway," "You are just a piece of garbage, and when people find that out, they will throw you away," "Hide your true self, it's not acceptable!" As I was beginning to acknowledge those words as lies, in my mind's eye I saw a picture of a trash heap. About a third of the way down the heap was a doll, or at least I thought it was a doll that had been thrown away. Sadly, as I zeroed in, I saw that the throwaway doll was me! Not only had I felt thrown away for most of my life, but I too threw myself away. Unfortunately, we tend to do to ourselves what has been done to us.

As I was willing to recognize those false beliefs as lies and not truth, I began to experience the deep pain in my heart they had caused. I wept for that little girl within me and realized that Jesus was weeping too, for He was described as a "man of sorrows and acquainted with grief" (Isaiah 53). He had also been "despised and rejected" and was depicted in those verses as "one from whom men hide their faces." That describes the way He too was shamed, so He was able to identify and weep with me. He had been through similar circumstances, so was able to connect with me in the pain, bringing healing and acceptance to that little one who, for a life-time, had felt thrown away. Then I had to join Him in re-nurturing myself with truth instead of lies. I had to cooperate with Jesus in the healing process instead of feeding the lies the "accuser of the brethren" (Revelations 12:10) had fed me all my life.

How do we feed the lies? One way they are fed is through our negative self-talk, when we beat ourselves up with words like, "Why are you so stupid?" We judge and condemn ourselves. Using our imagination to see ourselves badly or looking in the mirror and berating the one we see there are ways that cause us to cooperate with the work of the enemy in our lives. Perhaps he causes you to second guess everything you say or verbally beat yourself up as you replay various scenarios and interactions.

After my shame lie was revealed, I began to see that little girl within me with eyes of compassion and love, instead of with hatred and shame. This is another good time to get a picture of you as a child and begin the process of accepting that little one. As I looked at photos of myself, I saw a completely different child for the first time in years. I had always believed I was pathetic and ugly, but instead I found a wonderful little girl who was sweet, a child who just needed to be nurtured. As I began to cooperate with the Spirit in that re-nurturing work, the little girl began to grow again in so many of the ways she had been stuck. That caused more integration to happen within me.

Legitimate or Real Shame

There are things that we do that are real shame. For example, when we have legitimately caused pain to God and others, it is our shame that must be owned and brought to the cross for forgiveness in order to be released. We should feel shame when we put another down, judge them or treat them without respect. In that case it is something we've done that needs forgiveness.

In our present culture, especially some in the younger generation, seem to have lost the ability to feel legitimate shame. Far too often anything goes! However, our shame is illegitimate when we feel shame over ourselves as people, feeling unworthy, unacceptable, or like we don't measure up. Because of Jesus' sacrifice for us, we already are "accepted in the Beloved" (Ephesians 1:6 NKJV).

Contempt

Another sign that we might have a shame belief is our use of contempt. Contempt is poorly understood and is often used without our even knowing why we're using it or that we're using it at all. Contempt is disdain or lack of respect and can come out in sarcasm, a put-down or in joking at another's expense. Dan Allender in his powerful book, *The Wounded Heart*, unmasks the use of contempt in an amazing way. He explains that contempt diminishes our feelings of shame, deadens our longings to be wanted and enjoyed, provides for us an illusion of control, and distorts the real problem, which is sin.

Contempt can be used toward ourselves as put-down's, angry self-talk or even self-hatred. However, some are more prone to use it toward others in putting them down with sarcasm, humor, or a joke to zing them. Contempt can be recognized or heard in an attitude or tone of voice. "Like a madman shooting firebrands or deadly arrows, is a man who deceives his neighbor and says, 'I was only joking" (Proverbs 26:18,19). Contempt is a form of anger that is not clean because it doesn't always sound like anger, yet still wounds deeply.

There was a person in my life that treated me with contempt for years, but because I was so shame-based, I never recognized it. It wasn't until I began to deal with my illegitimate shame that I was able to feel the fiery darts of contempt. When we begin to recognize contempt and refuse to use or be recipients of it any longer, the fear of shame that might be driving it can begin to be revealed to us since shame and contempt work hand in hand. If contempt is covering over our longings, we can begin to identify them and reconnect with that deep part of us. Refusing to use contempt as a hiding place opens the door for a deeper work of God in our lives on the heart level.

Responsibility

Responsibility is another thing that can cause confusion in our lives. As with real and false shame, we sometimes haven't taken responsibility for what was really ours, such as when we've judged someone or haven't been faithful with our word, and instead we've taken false responsibility for others' feelings or actions. We might have done this by trying to protect them from consequences, disappointment, or pain. This can happen with our children when we try to cover for them, but it is often *our* pain or shame we're trying to protect them from, not theirs at all. So many times parents help too much with their children's homework or run to school with the forgotten lunch instead of allowing the children the freedom to fail so they can learn from their mistakes. I see now that when I did things like that, I was really doing it so I'd feel better. I was caretaking their feelings, but it really was about me.

Taking false responsibility can drive us to do things we don't have the grace for because we fear someone will be disappointed if we don't. In a case like that, we're taking responsibility for *their feelings* and, in effect, selling our soul for false peace or acceptance or so they won't be disappointed with us. There will be other times when we make a choice to lay down our desires for the sake of another, but that's a choice of love and not an obligation to take care of someone else's feelings. False responsibility can come out of being a "pleaser" and never wanting to disappoint or cause anyone to hurt. I did this in numerous ways for many years without realizing it because of the unhealed pain within me. Because of the wounds I carried, I tried to keep others from hurting and tried to protect them from living out what they needed to experience.

Our wonderfully wise heavenly Father gives His children the freedom to fail and, as a parent, it's important that we not to try to control or over-protect our children from the consequences they need to face. If children don't learn to take responsibility for their actions when they are little, there can be more severe consequences as they get older. We might find them as adults trapped in blaming others or blaming their circumstances every time they feel real shame for avoiding responsibility, still looking for someone to cover and take care of them. As my grandmother who had five children always used to say, "Little children, little problems, big children, big problems!" Let's deal with the problems while they are little.

Real Responsibility

True responsibility or the lack of it, can be seen in how we respect and honor others just because they are people created in God's image and likeness. It can also be seen in how we take responsibility for what is ours without using blame or avoidance to escape it. We need to own our mistakes and failures so forgiveness can flow from God to us and between each other.

In our culture, with its "me-centered" way of thinking, there is often no respect for another's time or property. There is a laxness developed toward keeping our word and our commitments. We can see that playing out in a common phrase we at times use far too glibly. "I'll call you…" is often said, but with no real intention of any follow-up. God is beginning to prick my heart whenever I say that and is helping me to see that if I don't follow through, it is a lack of integrity. We find doctors offices having to remind people when they have an appointment, but that was not the case in years past.

Many years ago in our country, there was integrity and a man's word was his bond. I believe God desires to heal us in this area. As we allow ourselves to begin to see the value of each person as He does, we will begin to treat others, their property, and time with respect. I just had a medical procedure done and afterward we got in a conversation with the doctor who shared that one of the most important things he learned from his father growing up was to treat all people with honor and respect. This is a doctor who is highly respected himself and has a reputation for his warmth and kindness. What a wonderfully wise, heart-connected father he had!

Questions to Ponder

Invite God to reveal any false guilt or shame you might be carrying, asking Him to surface any core false-shame beliefs that might be ruling your life without your knowledge.

Are you able to identify any areas of false responsibility that need to be released?

Are you able to identify any areas of real responsibility you might have been avoiding?

Ask God to reveal any ways you might have used self-protection to avoid real relationship or to keep the relationships you do have safe.

Make a list any people who have hurt you in the past or present. They are the ones that will be necessary to forgive if you are to move forward toward freedom.

Assignment

Separate any real guilt or shame from false guilt or shame by making a list with columns labeled:
Real Guilt   False Guilt   Real Shame   False Shame

Include in the list any false guilt or shame you might be carrying for someone else and silently give it back to it whomever it belongs.

Find a picture of yourself as a child at whatever age you might have experienced shame. Really see that little one, working with the picture until you can joyfully embrace him or her with all your heart.

Scripture

"Do not be afraid; you will not suffer shame. Do not fear disgrace; you will not be humiliated. You will forget the shame of your youth…" Isaiah 54:4

Receiving The Life of Jesus

If you have never really invited Jesus Christ to come into your life and take it over with the knowledge that you have been forgiven, I encourage you to take this opportunity to welcome Him in. He stands at the door of your heart and knocks as Revelation 3:20 reveals. He is simply waiting for your invitation. Your part is to open the door and welcome Him in just like you would do if He were knocking at the door of your home. Jesus knows you, has always known you and your deepest desires, knowing what will bring you the deepest joy.

"Jesus, I have often made a mess of things, I've wanted my own way (we *all* come short - Romans 3:23) *and I'm so sorry. Please forgive me and come into my life to take it over. You know me far better than I know myself. Thank you for dying for me on the cross and paying the price for new life for me."*

"For it is by grace you have been saved through faith - and this not from yourselves, it is the gift of God - not by works, so that no one can boast." Ephesians 2:8,9

"Yet to all who received him, to those who believed in his name, he gave the right to become children of God." John 1:12

Receiving Jesus opens the way to a personal relationship with God and gives us eternal life (John 17:3). To have that, John 3:3 tells us we must "born again". In inviting Jesus to take over our lives, we are born again and our lives are changed.

7
YOUR VOICE

Hindrances to Developing Your Voice, Your Voice in Marriage, God-Given Boundaries

*"Simply let your 'Yes' be 'Yes', and your 'No,' 'No';
anything beyond this comes from the evil one."*
Matthew 5:37

God has given you your voice for a reason. It's part of your identity, part of what makes you, you! Your voice matters because you matter. It is meant to express your heart, your wisdom, and your wonderful, unique gifts, even if you don't yet know what they are. Your God-given voice is as valuable as anyone else's; no more, no less. There are treasures God has planted within each of us, but too often they either get dismissed as not valuable or they've never been discovered. We sometimes look at those who are more intelligent, educated, polished, and eloquent as having more to offer and, too many times, that lie causes us to shrink back. Yes, others might have learned to flow better with their gifts, but we can't begin to treasure or develop what we have dismissed.

As an encouragement to you, I will honestly share that it would never have entered my mind to write a book. I didn't believe I had anything to say or the abilities necessary to even entertain such a thought. As you might be picking up, I never paid much attention in English class because I foolishly judged it as a waste of time. Little did I know that a decision made way back then would cause this to be so much more difficult today!

Twenty years ago, I began writing letters to God every day, hashing through my emotional struggles by honestly sharing my heart with Him. Doing that produced not only healing, but an intimacy between us that He used to bring forth new ways of seeing, and along with that, began to show me the gifts that were locked within. It takes courage to step out into any unknown venture, but first I had to believe that He was calling me to do this and that I had something of value to bring. Writing this book has been a vulnerable experience, but I have felt His encouragement all through the task in so many little ways. When we begin to accept the truth that we each carry gifts that are needed by others, we can start to co-labor with God's Spirit in the process of developing and releasing them. The interesting thing is that it might not even resemble our picture! For example, my call and gifts are to see captives set free, so it doesn't matter if God chooses to do that through counseling, speaking, writing, or over coffee with a friend.

Let me give you an example of the robbery I experienced throughout my life. Not only couldn't I imagine I had anything to say in a book, but due to painful, embarrassing experiences as a child in a Sunday school play, I was also unable to speak in public. My brain and mouth would freeze. Part of what paralyzed me was my family's criticism over anyone who did speak. I can remember making a vow that I would never allow myself to be judged like that. Fortunately, the enemy's robbery I had experienced became more and more evident as my desire to be used by God grew. This caused me to cry out to God for more freedom. I had to allow Jesus to go back to that young girl who needed healing from the embarrassing experience of the past, receive it, break the vow, and forgive my family. As I did that, I began to have the freedom to step out in areas that were formerly terrifying.

Have you been robbed? God hates robbery (Isaiah 61:8). He doesn't hate you; He hates the robbery you've experienced. He hates the thief, Satan who destroys (John 10:10) so He came to destroy the works of the enemy (1 John 3:8). We are here on purpose for a purpose and there are treasures within us all that have not yet been uncovered! Your treasures are different than mine, unique to you alone, but they are needed just as your life is needed; that's why the enemy has tried so hard to destroy you.

We all have the longing to be seen, heard, and truly known even with all our flaws and shortcomings, yet still be accepted, wanted, and enjoyed. Those are the longings we are born with. Too often as children we found ourselves mocked, ignored, not heard or even perhaps downright rejected. If we aren't seen or heard growing up, it becomes easy to distance ourselves from our desires, since they never seemed very important to anyone else.

"Before I was born the Lord called me, from my birth He made mention of my name. He made my mouth like a sharpened sword..." (Isaiah 49:1,2). My mouth, my voice is needed, as is yours. The enemy also desires to use our voice, but Jesus reminds us that it's out of the heart that our mouth speaks, so when our heart has been surrendered to Him, we have something of His life to bring forth through our own uniqueness – something that is needed by others. We won't do it perfectly because we are all just in the process of being conformed to His image, but staying sensitive to His correction, however it comes, will help our hearts and voices to be purified.

As mentioned before, I've been writing letters to God from my heart for almost a quarter of a century, but something new is happening. After I write, He responds, sometimes with revelation, sometimes loving affirmation, and sometimes with gentle correction and clarification. I never feel condemned or judged, but always accepted and loved by His caring discipline. Those whom He loves, He gently disciplines (Hebrews 12:4-13).

Hinderances to Developing Our Voice

Sometimes, in homes where there is a controlling parent, a child never really develops his voice. Everyone thinks for him so no one helps him discover who he is and what he really thinks.

Before long the child begins to doubt himself, his abilities and his worth. We all want to know if we have what it takes. When a parent controls a child, the conclusion he can come to is that he's lacking. Sometimes a child has a parent who talks incessantly so everyone else in the family gives up speaking altogether. A different child might get an angry, rebellious voice, fight against the parent, and sometimes grow up to be an overbearing, controlling adult who knows it all.

In any case, God's precious gift of the true voice of the heart was robbed. When we were not heard in the past, it's not unusual to give up trying to speak and just bury our voice. In some cases, we might even become an adult woman with a little girl voice. I can think of several women like that and, before I understood this, I wondered why they spoke that way. As their healing progressed, I listened as their little girl voice matured and they spoke with new authority.

Sometimes we might have made a vow that goes something like this: "No one ever listens to me anyway, so why even bother to talk and give my opinion?" I used to hide my voice because I believed I had nothing of value to say so people would laugh at me if I spoke. Some go the opposite way and continually give their opinion and advice to prove they're worth listening to. Then there are those who just try to keep the peace by swallowing their voice to avoid conflict, controversy or an explosion. I've counseled many people who have chosen false peace, or what some call peace, at any cost. This is simply an illusion of peace, carrying with it a huge cost in the loss of their true self.

Jesus told us that He didn't come to bring "peace, but a sword" and warned it could cause problems in one's own household (Matthew 10:34-37). Why? Because to gain true peace, we sometimes have to engage in a measure of conflict or, at the very least, be willing to use our voice and accept the reality that we won't always agree, but we can still have unity in our diversity.

Conflict doesn't have to be a bad thing, but when we've grown up in a home where conflicts were never resolved, we might have made a vow to avoid them at all costs. Vows have to be released and we need to repent of them because they will imprison us. Letting them go opens the way for the freedom to be able to love Jesus and His ways more than we love our false safety and peace. When false peace rules, instead of laying down our life for Jesus, we are laying it down for the absence of conflict and the pretense of relationship. That avoidance of conflict can sometimes come from a deeply hidden fear of abandonment. We might have a fear that if we use our voice, we won't be approved of and if we aren't approved of, we'll be abandoned and left alone as unacceptable. Rejection and abandonment might have been something you experienced as a child that has continued to hold you captive in the present. Until that's healed, there can be an unhealthy fear of man instead of a healthy fear of God.

For our relationships to be healthy, each person is needed to be alive and present. Otherwise, one dominates and the other hides producing no real relationship at all since both must be involved to have real connection. Truly loving the person we are in relationship with might require our willingness to speak even when the other doesn't like it, however our goal is to attempt to always "speak the truth in love" (Ephesians 4:15). We need to be willing to love the person more than we love the relationship with that person.

What might that look like? Sometimes it will require us to use our voice in a truthful, loving way that brings discomfort or temporary upset to the relationship. The woman, who began to stand up to her husband's frequent explosions toward her, really loved her husband well through her unwillingness to be his scape-goat. That eventually caused him to face his own anger, though for a season there was much conflict. Far too often, we do not love the person well at all, but just want to keep the peace and the illusion we've created.

When we think we love someone by remaining silent, we're really just loving ourselves in a selfish manner and trying to keep our own world intact. For example, as parents we can think we love our children well when we try to cover their mistakes, but too many times we're protecting ourselves by keeping our own world looking good. We can think we love them well when we give them lots of things, but what they really long for is connection with our hearts. They want us to see them, to desire to know them as they are not how we want them to be.

Jesus gives us the freedom to fail and then, when we do, He never abandons us, but walks with us lovingly helping us to pick up the pieces. He doesn't just fix things, He rebuilds on His new foundation when we allow Him.

Ignoring our heart's desires long enough can cause us to no longer feel them and if we do, we distance from them or begin to hate them. We feel it hurts too much to long and feels far better to settle. Then we often try to find a way to perform well so people will see the value we bring and, at the very least, need us. Because of that we have often developed need-based relationships instead of love-based relationships. Need-based relationships are co-dependent, unhealthy relationships that cause us to find people to take care of or, the reverse, we quietly demand to be taken care of by others. Lori had a collection of people who always needed her. She seldom had time for the genuine needs of her family because she was always putting out fires for all the ones who were pulling on her. Lori complained about it, but in reality, she enjoyed feeling needed and used that to gain a false identity. The lie of that false identity said, "I am the one who is needed, people can't get along without me, so that gives me worth."

We are meant to enjoy a variety of relationships that encourage, value, and sharpen one another. However, there are seasons when God allows others to be sandpaper for us and us for them for His specific purposes in each of our lives. A close friend and I were sandpaper for each other during a particularly difficult healing time. Although it was certainly not a comfortable season, much good came out of it and our friendship was actually strengthened. There will also be some people God puts in our lives for a period of time, special ones to care for and mentor with the goal of helping them grow up into their own dependency upon God. When we begin to fill God's role by meeting their needs ourselves, we are keeping them as children dependent on us and not loving them well.

There is a difference between being a caregiver and a caretaker. A caretaker assumes false responsibility for the other person and creates a false dependency on the caretaker. It develops a use relationship with each using the other to meet their own needs. Hidden beneath the surface can be the belief that if we are needed, we won't be left all alone. A caregiver gives care where needed and with wisdom helps the other to learn to care for themselves in a healthy way by depending on God. Early on, I didn't understand that necessary truth and experienced much burn-out because of trying to meet everyone's needs. In that case, we can be driven by human compassion instead of the compassion that comes from God.

It has been my experience that if we care for hurting people in a loving, healthy way and refuse to get pulled on with their demands, they will eventually learn to depend on God instead of us. That's where we have to learn to have a clear "no" without being double-minded, wavering or having false guilt when we feel them trying to pull from us. We have to be willing to allow them to be unhappy with us without trying to fix them, or falling under feelings of rejection when they get angry because we haven't done things their way. If we do feel rejected, that can be a sign that we have more rejection from our past yet to be healed.

It is most important to remember that Jesus is their healer, not us. Our part is to be consistent in loving them well even when they don't seem lovable. Understanding that God sometimes wounds us in order to heal is a principle we have to learn if we are going to be free to allow people to experience their pain without trying to fix them. "For he wounds, but he also binds up; he injures, but his hands also heal" (Job 5:18). Like a good surgeon going after the cancer in our bodies, God often does the same.

I know from the experience of having had cancer myself that the wounding can bring pain in order for healing to come. I felt fine prior to surgery even though there was a cancer within that was silently bringing destruction to my body. After the surgery, instead of feeling better, I felt terrible for a while until the process of healing was finally completed. That process gave me back my life and the same can be true with emotional wounding and healing.

Our Voice in Marriage

In marriage, either partner can lose their voice. Then one spouse will dominate, control, and make most of the decisions, perhaps even speaking for their partner with others. One woman had a very strong, overbearing husband who enjoyed being in control, but participated very little in the day-to-day happenings and responsibilities of the family. Because this woman had a fear of abandonment, she silently carried the heavy load of doing everything herself, but inside got more and more resentful toward her husband. As she began to face her anger and fears to finally get her voice, she shared her feelings with her husband who got quite angry at first because the world he built was shaking. Within a short time, however, he quietly began to help and little by little he began respecting and enjoying his wife in new ways that were impossible while she remained silent.

Far too often in marriages one remains silent in order to keep the peace, which on the surface appears to be a good reason. When this happens long enough, the silent partner begins to believe they really don't have anything of value to say or, because of a fear of loss, they choose to remain silent. A deep resentment can often begin to build on both sides. This sometimes causes the silent partner to lead a sneaky life on the side by keeping things from the dominate partner, emotionally separating the couple even further. The silent partner might shop then hide their purchases, lie about the places they go, or report lower earnings to the dominate partner. Through the secrecy, the intimacy they long for gets sabotaged. If healing in the relationship is to come, both partners need to be open and honest with each other in order to bring the necessary changes. It's easy to put blame on the dominating one, but the silent one took the easy way out by losing their voice. Real change takes openness, honesty, courage, understanding, and vulnerability on both sides. The most difficult person to be vulnerable with can be our own spouse because we have the most to lose in that relationship.

I have heard many a dominating, controlling wife say she wished her husband would stand up to her and have a voice. However, when he does, the reality is she fights him for all she's worth! If that controlling pattern is to break, it will take the courage of the husband to enter the war. Of course, it could go the other way as well, with the husband as the controller and the wife remaining silent. When we're dealing with domination, we must see it is a spirit of control that needs to be warred against. The fight isn't against the person, but against the survival system they are using to hide themselves in. In entering the war, you are actually fighting for the real person, but without their survival system. Husbands have told me they didn't like it when their wives finally got a voice and stood up to them, but after they got over the shock and stopped being so threatened by it, they loved and respected their wives so much more.

Domination, manipulation, and intimidation are all forms of control that kill true relationship. They create fear-based relationships instead of love-based ones and are a yoke of bondage for all concerned. "It is for freedom that Christ has set us free. Stand firm then, and do not let yourselves be burdened again by a yoke of slavery." (Galatians 5:1) To keep us from getting selfish in our relating, verse 13 adds, "You, my brothers, were called to be free. But do not use your freedom to indulge the sinful nature, rather, serve one another in love." Anytime we obey any form of a spirit of control, we are voluntarily giving up the freedom that Jesus paid for.

Many years ago, we were involved in a business relationship where intimidation and manipulation were used. Anytime this man didn't get his way, he would use an outburst of anger to try to force us into backing away from our opinion and complying with his. It was messy, but we had to stand up to him if the relationship was to continue and as that happened, he backed down.

Having a voice, especially in marriage, can also help us learn how to communicate in a way that is not accusatory, but is based on "I feel..." instead of "You always..." The latter causes the other person to become defensive, but the former just simply shares heart-felt feelings.

Something also needs to be said for men and women being created as help-opposites. Being an opposite sometimes feels like a bad thing because we desire others to believe, think, and act as we do. It's peaceful that way, but then we don't stretch, grow or see the whole picture since we are so similar. One couple I admire greatly seemed to be total opposites in all ways when they got married, except for in their core values and love for the Lord. They were actually both quite extreme in their opposite ways, which was not particularly healthy. It looked like the marriage would be a disaster and probably would have been if they both had not been submitted to God. Because of that commitment, Jesus was able to bring them to a much healthier middle ground, more so than many marriages ever achieve. However, it took tremendous struggle between them to get there and it wasn't always pretty.

That's where our commitment to God to build together is so necessary since we might not *feel* too committed to our partner at that point. We must face how disappointed we have been, sometimes many times over, if we are ever to move toward heart forgiveness. It helps to remember that we believe God brought us together in the first place and as we become willing to walk it through with trust in Him, He can tear down what needs to be torn down in both parties. We are meant to be opposite halves of a whole. Opposites are often opposing, but it wasn't meant to be that way. God has created husbands and wives to fit together in the midst of their opposing views, thoughts, and opinions. One should not drown-out or dominate the other, but each should contribute their own particular way of seeing. Both sides are needed to see the whole picture.

Learning to live together as opposites is something I am still in the process of walking out and not always doing very well! When we are willing to struggle through the conflict without each demanding our own way, there is often a wisdom that is produced, bringing us to a healthy, balanced viewpoint. If there is a major decision to be made, it can be a time for each to share their viewpoint, pray for God's wisdom and timing, and then wait for the Spirit to bring both into the one accord that can only come from Him. My husband and I have experienced this on several major moves. Years ago, I felt God showing me we were going to make a major move to Florida, but my husband didn't see that at the time. As we held it in prayer and waited ten years, God revealed to my husband that, yes, it was time to make that move. Since the timing of things is so very important, we are urged through the scriptures to desire to understand the "times and seasons" and not to move ahead of God's timing (Acts 17:26,27).

When faced with an opposing opinion, we often get defensive, feel threatened, and feel we have to defend our way of seeing. What would happen if we could listen to each other for the wisdom that might be there without feeling threatened? Is there a middle ground we could find as we struggle through together? When we don't find that middle ground, our opposing views usually get more deeply entrenched; we become unmoving and very self-protective of our own way. I am finding that for me, it is taking a lifetime of marriage to begin to get to this middle ground, but since God created us to be dependent on Him, we are unable to do even that without His help. In fact, seeing the reality of how God intended for us to marry an opposite is something I have only begun to grasp in the past few years. So many fear they made a mistake in marrying such an opposite personality and yet, when I ask them if they believe God originally brought them together, they say, "Yes, I think so." If that is so and if we weren't acting out of total rebellion in choosing a mate, could this be God's way of sanctifying us? (Philippians 2:12,13)

In order to get to a healthy, loving, balanced relationship, we have to grieve our past disappointments regarding our spouse. There were far too many times when my husband and I didn't work through our opposing views very well and we each were hurt. When that hurt gets buried, it can grow into a seeping resentment toward the one we once loved. In fact, if we're truly honest, we can almost begin to hate the one we loved. God understands that dynamic because the scripture tells us that Israel, the one He loved, He also hated (Jeremiah 12:7,8). Hatred is not the absence of love, although the enemy would like to make us think it is. Satan whispers, "How could you possibly have any love for the one you feel such hatred toward now?"

One way out is to begin to face our deeply disappointed pictures. There are usually things over the years that we desired to be different. Facing them honestly would probably require us to admit we were deeply hurt on many occasions. This is true for both partners. If we will face how disappointed we have been, and begin to grieve the losses we have felt throughout our years together, a way can be made to truly release each other from our judgments. As that happens, love begins to rise up once again from the bottom of the barrel and there can be a richness and open honesty of relationship that comes out of it. For all honest marriages though, there are good seasons and not so good ones. That's why the old wedding ceremony contained the commitment that marriage was "for better or for worse." "Love never ends" – it endures (1 Corinthians 13RSV). It also must be stated though, that abuse in a marriage from either partner is never acceptable.

Sadly, for anyone who has had abuse in their past, their choice of a mate is too often someone who is either passive or in some way abusive. One woman was more or less content with her emotionally absent husband even though she never deeply respected him. Once she began healing from the horror of her past abuse, she recognized a desire growing within her for the two of them to connect emotionally, but of course he couldn't because of his own wounding. It was at that point she realized that if he didn't begin to look at his own life and what was shutting him down emotionally, their marriage would be in trouble because she was no longer able to live in pretense. Fortunately, as her husband saw her growth and freedom, he began to long to experience the same for himself so he was willing to take the action needed to become whole.

As we begin to heal within ourselves from the past abuse, we begin to desire healthier, more alive relationships with each partner respecting the other. As we begin to recognize those desires, it's not unusual to become discouraged, but there is hope in seeing that God is a healer. He can restore each of us to His original blueprint for our lives when we will allow Him, so neither partner has to remain wounded. However, it will take honest, open, loving communication with each other as well as dependence on God instead of depending on our old self-protective ways of relating. There is often a reluctance to share honestly for fear of hurting the other. Even when we "speak the truth in love" (Ephesians 4:15) as the Bible tells us we must, some hurt is inevitable. However, we should consider what our motivation is for sharing. Is my motivation to truly love my spouse, becoming closer with a more intimate relationship, and seeing him experience more freedom? Or is my motivation to harm him? Before sharing, we must establish that we're not trying to harm through revenge or punishment, but that our motivation is to love them well for their sake. Jesus wounds us in order to bring healing, but His intention is never to harm us.

There is another way I am learning to embrace my husband and our opposite ways of seeing. He is a detail-oriented person, which comes forth in his wonderful talent as an artist. His career has been so successful due in part to his attention to detail, but at the same time that can make him painfully slow with various tasks. On the other hand, I am a big-picture person, a visionary, and I generally move very quickly. As we put those two opposite natures together, it can cause stress and frequent misunderstandings in our natural selves. However, after fifty years of marriage, I am finally beginning to learn that his attention to detail has prevented me from making some hasty mistakes and he's beginning to see that my big-picture vision has stretched him to see in larger, healthier ways. In finances, I tend to rush through the details so I can get to what I deem as *really important!* Fortunately for me, Bruce has caught my simple math mistakes and has saved the day on more than one occasion. On the other hand, he could be quite content with never straying far from home, yet many times he's been willing to go places for my sake. Very often on the way home, he has commented that he was glad we went because it caused him to see life from a different perspective. Opposites need each other!

As you can see, we've been very slow learners! Our opposite natures reveal just how much we all need Jesus to help us work with His Spirit instead of in agreement with the accuser of the brethren, who wants to steal, kill, and destroy true unity in marriages. Unity is not conformity, but simply allowing God to bring both to a new way of seeing, which is His way. The wonderful thing is that we *can* have unity in our diversity!

As I look back in hindsight over my child-rearing days, I can see what I couldn't see back then. There were times when I thought my husband was being too harsh with our boys when I wanted to be softer and vice versa, so that we often opposed each other. Sadly, that happened far too many times and I can understand now why both parents are necessary. One or the other doesn't have all the answers or the right way of doing things. I can see now there was truth coming from both of us and, if we had learned then to work better together, our boys would have benefited greatly.

The more confidence we have in how God has made us and the gifts that we each individually carry, the more we will release those gifts. Our voice is a gift that we use to release our piece, adding it to the pieces of others. It's not about being right or the fear of being wrong, but simply adding your part to the whole. You are needed and your voice is needed, otherwise God would not have given you one. Your voice expresses your heart, your wisdom, and your way of seeing. It is as valuable as any other's; no more, no less.

For years, I didn't speak and share my opinions because fear told me I had nothing to say. If I risked saying anything, I was sure my ignorance would be laughed at. The fear of experiencing shame kept me prisoner. When the healing from my shame-lie finally came, my speaking wasn't very fluent because I had rarely used my voice in the past. It's interesting to me that I never had trouble using my voice in the home; it was outside of the home that the fear of shame kept me quiet. When I finally realized I had a piece to bring, it released me to begin to honor God by taking the risk. Are we people of courage or are we hiding our light under a bushel because it's safer that way? If we are going to experience the wind of God in our sails, we have to stop hugging the shore.

To lose our voice is to lose our personality and, ultimately, our identity. It's out of our identity that the purposes for which we have been created can be fulfilled. We can see now why the enemy tries so hard to destroy us and our voice. "For we are God's workmanship, created in Christ Jesus to do good works, which God prepared in advance for us to do" (Ephesians 2:10). These works come out of who we are, out of our identity, and not apart from the true us. They are the works He is preparing us to do. Not everything is our responsibility. Sometimes we jump in because there is a need, not waiting to see if there is someone else God has prepared to meet it. This happens far too often when churches try to find people to fill slots, instead of waiting for the one God has purposed to meet that need.

Sometimes, the need we determine to be so great is not to be met at all because God is doing something else in that situation and, if we jump in to fill it, we can find ourselves working against the purposes of God. In one church, the pastor would get annoyed because the people wouldn't cooperate in doing the things he determined needed to be done in order for his vision to be fulfilled. Instead of waiting for God to bring the right person at the right time, if that indeed was God's vision too, the pastor placed people in positions they had no gifts or maturity for. Sadly, many were serving through the guilt they felt the pastor putting on them and the fear that things would fall apart if they didn't cooperate. Until we get an understanding of God's timing and His ways and are willing to wait on Him, we too often play god in many situations. Very often we give our hands in good works, but they are disconnected from our true hearts and the way He has made us to flow.

You have something to say and the world needs the piece you bring. None of us has the whole pie; we each only have a piece. However, the true piece you have to bring comes out of the deepest part of you because that's where God has placed His treasures. The treasures and gifts that are uniquely yours will come out of your particular personality, be connected to the history of your individual life including the pain that has been redeemed, and will be released as resurrected life and broken bread to feed others. Too many times we bring forth truth from our minds, but it has never been broken into our hearts. When we are very intelligent, it's easy to devour books and understand them intellectually, but still be unable to walk out those particular truths. I know those who have taught classes that way and, although a lot of knowledge is obtained by those listening, the people are not impacted on any deep level of the heart. Their minds are tickled, but it's out of the heart that people are fed on a deeper level.

We can have all those wonderful treasures within, but without the freedom of using our voice, we will not be able to release them, others will not be able to fully enjoy us, and we won't love them well. If our mouth is like that sharpened sword Isaiah 49 speaks of, then our voice under the direction of God's Spirit can cut through darkness and bring light and life to the world around us. If we are to be used like that, then we must be willing to value our own voice and the particular piece we bring as something entrusted to us by God for the benefit of building His Kingdom. In the Lord's Prayer, Jesus urges us to pray that His kingdom would be on earth as it is in heaven (Matthew 6:10). We each have a part to play as we co-labor with God in bringing forth His kingdom purposes on the earth!

Boundaries

At this point though, a word must be spoken about God-given boundaries. These boundaries are a necessary part of having our voice. Unlike the impenetrable walls we build within to cover and protect ourselves, boundaries are given by God, come from His authority within, and are meant to be flexible. In a healthy home, boundaries are learned in childhood, but in dysfunctional families, personal boundaries are often trampled over and stolen from us. This happens especially when there was abuse of any kind. An excellent source to obtain understanding of personal boundaries is the book entitled, *Boundaries* by Dr. Henry Cloud and Dr. John Townsend.

When our boundaries have been violated and lost, we may build a wall around our hearts as a self-protective way of preventing ourselves from being used again and hurt by others. This wall can be built out of anger or fear. We close ourselves in with fortresses of self-protection even though behind the wall we feel lonely and isolated. We might have many relationships, but the relationships are usually superficial and don't touch our hearts on any deep level of connection. We might avoid relationships because of the fear of being used or consumed by others or be driven by the false shame of being discovered as having nothing of value if others were to fully see and know us. The fortress of self-protection might have the illusion of keeping us safe, but we can feel miserably alone behind the wall we built.

I remember when I first became aware of the isolation I felt within the fortress I had created. No one got close enough to hurt me because I had deadened my heart and walled it off a long time earlier. People would tell me they didn't know me, but I had no idea what they were talking about. It finally took the realization of my loneliness, isolation and the longing to be free to drive me to cry out desperately to God for healing. That began the process of my own journey. I remember a woman whom I really desired to get to know, but you could actually see the shades being drawn down over her eyes whenever anyone got too close. She was always very superficially friendly and pleasant, but closed down. When I mentioned it, she wasn't even aware of what she was doing or why.

If we try to come out of hiding without having healthy boundaries, others have the opportunity to trample us, dump their garbage on us and use us for their own agendas. No wonder we wall ourselves in! Boundaries are simply personal space around our personality, similar to a house with a fenced-in yard that has a gate. When you come to me, my gate is open to you unless you plan on dumping your garbage all over my yard. That garbage could come in the form of control, blame, shaming, contemptuous words, use or abuse of any kind. If that begins to happen, I will have to close my gate to you until you can come in and treat me with respect. I will welcome talking about whatever the issues might be, but it must be done with each of us honoring the other. I choose not to build a wall against you, but I have the right to close my gate if I am feeling used, abused or not respected. You have the same God-given privilege.

Boundaries give us an ability to have intimacy, but at the same time, prevent being wrongly used for the agendas and purposes of others. If we don't have them, it's possible to end up having our will overrun. Too many have dismissed themselves and don't understand they have the right to say no (Mathew 5:37). God gives us that right, but cautions us not to be double-minded when we say it. There will be times when you will need quality time for yourself and family, when you have other things to do or when you just don't wish to participate in something. Many people feel compelled to say yes even though they don't want to, because they believe they must. They feel trapped into going where they are invited, but their heart is resentful and when they do go, they are not really present. Unless the Spirit of God is nudging you to go for some reason of His own, you have the right to say, "Thank you, perhaps another time," or whatever would be kind, but still be a firm no. However, we cannot be double minded with the fear of man or, as the scripture says, we will be driven like the wind (James 1:6-8). It is not necessary to have what we might think of as a valid excuse, so there is no need for a lengthy explanation, just kindness. If the other doesn't accept that, they are most likely trying to pull you along with their agenda which is not healthy for either person.

Sometimes people have a false loyalty that doesn't permit them to say no. Loyalty is a wonderful quality, but there are times when it is not a healthy loyalty for either person. Remember, "It is for freedom that Christ has set us free. Stand firm, then, and do not let yourselves be burdened again by a yoke of slavery." (Galatians 5:1) To obey man out of the fear of having to keep them pleased with us is bondage or slavery. However, to keep from falling into selfishness, let's always remember to serve one another in love, but never from fear (Galatians 5:13). Serving one another in love must come out of a free heart because we are not really free to serve them well until we can say no. We are to be directed by God's Spirit and not by the fear of man.

Let me share a word of caution that I learned the hard way. We can sometimes put more value on those outside our families than we do on our own loved ones. How many moms are available for every good cause, for every person who demands their time, all at the expense of their own families? How many husbands or wives have chosen to value careers over recognizing the needs of their own families, often justifying it by saying they are just providing. In one family, the husband chose to devote a tremendous amount of time to his career. There were many times when he wasn't available for family activities or to bring balance to his wife for the sake of the children. Sadly, the children grew up without dad's regular presence so some of the things that got out of balance were never corrected. As a result, all members of the family experienced robbery. They had many things, but it mattered little in the bigger picture.

Remember it's the thief, Satan, who wants to steal, kill, and destroy (John 10:10), especially families. When we don't love ourselves in a healthy way, we will often neglect our families for the sake of others' needs and value our outside interests more. When our families are neglected in that way, especially when it's out of "service for the Lord," resentment is often produced, not only toward us, but many times toward God as well.

When the hurts of life come, it becomes easy to erect a self-protective covering over our heart. Sadly, self-protection is a barrier to the very love we long to give and receive that can be subtly erected when we have been wounded in a relationship. One of two things sometimes happens when we get deeply hurt. We will either self-protect our hearts by hiding them behind a wall or we will continue to foolishly trust someone who is not trustworthy at that point. When our hearts have been fully entrusted to God, He gives the discernment and wisdom to live in this broken world. If we are hurt, we have the promise that "in all things God works for the good of those who love him, who have been called according to his purpose" (Romans 8:28). Only God is able to take what the enemy meant for evil and work it for our good. God is a Redeemer, a Restorer, and a Repairer. Only He can take what was subtracted from us, restore us, heal us and then multiply the restoration through us out to others.

The Scriptures tell us we are to love our neighbor as we love ourselves (Matthew 22:39). Protecting ourselves is the opposite of loving, but having healthy boundaries enable us to love ourselves along with others. When we love ourselves, we don't love ourselves more then others, but simply as much as we love others. We are one of the others, but too often, we treat ourselves as a non-person, giving others more value and worth than we give to ourselves, or else we close them out altogether. We will never love others well if we don't love ourselves in a healthy way. "This is love; not that we loved God, but that He loved us and sent His Son as an atoning sacrifice for our sins. Dear friends, since God so loved us, we also ought to love one another." (1 John 4:10,11) Notice from these verses that love begins in the heart of God and extends to us. Then, as we truly begin to receive it into our hearts and not just our minds alone, that love very naturally outflows from our hearts to others.

If we are to be healthy with good relationships, boundaries are absolutely necessary. They are something we must teach our children as well so they will recognize use or abuse when it comes. Boundaries are part of learning to respect and honor another as well as ourselves because we are all made in the image of God and are to be treated with love and respect.

Questions to Ponder

How might I have diminished or lost my voice, thinking it's not as valuable as the voices of others?

How might I have tried to control others through dominating, manipulating, or intimidating? Which tactic seems to be the strongest? Why?

What do I feel when others don't agree with me? Does it cause me to either get angry or desire to shut down? Why?

What might be the "piece" that God has given me to bring to others? If I don't know, what do I currently do that seems to bring life to myself and to others?

Which do I have: healthy boundaries with gates, or walls built around my heart to keep others out and to keep myself feeling safe and protected?

Assignment

If you have lost your voice, ask God for an opportunity to begin to speak out with a person who feels safe. When we've lost our voice, it takes practice to get it back.

If God shows you that you've been controlling, the next time
you are tempted, don't! If you stop doing something you feel
compelled to do, the particular fear the control is covering can
begin to surface.

Scripture

"It is for freedom that Christ has set us free. Stand firm then and do
not let yourselves be burdened again by a yoke of slavery. 13.
"You, my brothers, were called to be free. But do not use your
freedom to indulge the sinful nature; rather, serve one another
in love." Galations 5:1

8
OUR SURVIVAL SYSTEMS

Our Hiding Places and Idols

"...for we have made a lie our refuge and falsehood our hiding place." Isaiah 28:15

L ife can be difficult. From early childhood many of us have struggled with disappointed longings because far too many times, the things we desired didn't happen. The people we wanted to accept and include us sometimes didn't. It feels bad enough when this happens at school or in the neighborhood, but can be devastating when it happens to a child in their own home. From early childhood, I developed survival systems, as many of us do, to cover the disappointed desires of wanting to belong. Those systems were how I survived at the time, because even in my own family, I felt on the outside looking in. One system was to tell myself that if I didn't really care about the ones I longed to accept me, it wouldn't hurt so much. Of course, it was a lie so all it really did was deaden my heart. Another way I killed desire was to prepare myself to expect the worst so if anything good happened it would be a surprise. If not, I was already prepared for the inevitable disappointment.

Sadly those systems took away the life of my heart and with it my hope and God-given desires. Desire connects to passion and without passion we are shut down and dull inside; just existing, never really living from the heart. Your issues might not have been the same as mine so the systems you used to survive could look very different. Since they all prevent us from living the life we desire, my hope is this will help you to recognize yours as well.

If we take an honest look at our lives, there were moments, even in our best relationships, when we felt misunderstood, disregarded, forgotten, or rejected in the midst of living everyday life. How have we made it through without our hearts being crushed by the disappointments and stresses we experienced? We've developed systems or ways of coping. There is built within us, even as children, the will to survive and we will do whatever it takes to make it through with at least the appearance of life. When our real self has felt rejected or not accepted we will often develop a false self to present to the world.

One woman's system or false self was efficiency. She was on top of everything, anticipating any problem before it ever happened. When coming from a healthy heart this can be a good quality, but because it was from her self-protective heart covering, it caused those around her to react with fear instead of love. She kept everyone on their toes, but connected to no one's heart. Those around her respected her, but feared her and she was left living in a lonely, isolated world of her own making. Thankfully, she has begun a wonderful journey of healing and is beginning to find her true self, connecting to others in new ways.

In his book *Wild at Heart*, John Eldredge puts it this way, "From the place of our woundedness we construct a false self. We find a few gifts that work for us, and we try to live off them." For some, their gifts have led them to become super-achievers, performing well to prove themselves. Some like me might have taken the opposite road to become under-achievers, never trying very hard at anything. Doing that guaranteed we would never be discovered as the failure we believed ourselves to be. Others may have chosen instead to cover the pain with a variety of things like addictions or compulsions. Another survival system that so many use is avoidance and procrastination because of the hope that if the person or problem is avoided and ignored, maybe it will go away.

Let's look at the survival system of addiction for a minute. We often think only of the obvious addictions like drugs, alcohol, the Internet, sex, and perhaps gambling. Yet seemingly good things like work, perfectionism, food, TV, books, computer games, sports, people and some of our relationships can be addictions. As Christians, we can use the Bible and religion to hide ourselves in. Sometimes, you can even hear a religious spirit rise up as a person's voice changes when they are praying or talking about God. They no longer just sound as they normally do, but a false piety takes over. As Christians, a religious spirit can become an acceptable way to hide ourselves, but that usually just makes others want to turn away from us. It doesn't draw anyone to God, only to religion. We may sometimes use a system of blame, just as Adam and Eve did, to hide in and keep from taking responsibility for our own actions and choices by playing the victim. There might have been a time when we were the victim of some cruel act, but when we hold onto that system in order to survive, we will never grow or heal. We will remain emotionally and relationally stunted, often sabotaging our future.

It always amazes me how a person can perform so well in their career, gain great success in their field, but still be so unable to relationally connect with others in a healthy way. One man was fairly well-known and widely acclaimed in his career. He was excellent at what he did, but was unable to connect with his wife, children, or those around him on any significant heart level. He often removed himself emotionally from deep discussions, especially those pertaining to disappointments or the revealing of actual feelings. He had an opinion about everything, but those opinions came from his head and not his heart. It left his family hungry, devoid of any real, satisfying relationship with him, and somewhat resentful because of the loss. They longed to know him, really know him. Fortunately for them, he recognized his fear and avoidance of past pain and began the slow process of healing and rediscovering his own heart. Even though he's still on his own journey, he's a much more content person with increasingly more fulfilling relationships.

Losing our own heart can happen when we refuse to face the relational pain that is still lodged deep within, often going way back to childhood. We can mature intellectually, but remain dwarfed emotionally and relationally so that more and more our intellect or career becomes a hiding place. Sadly, we will often grow in the areas that are easiest for us to develop while ignoring the others in which we feel the most potential for shame. For some who are naturally spiritually minded, their system can often be seen playing out in the spiritual arena. For many years before facing my own emotional pain and beginning on my particular healing journey, my energy went into developing my spirit. Unfortunately, I've known far too many others who have done that as well.

Having an intense spiritual hunger that began in childhood, once I came into a relationship with Jesus it was extremely easy to develop the appearance of spiritual growth. I loved the Bible and became a Bible trivia whiz. Of course, it was applauded in the church so no one bothered to see that the rest of my life and relationships were a mess. Like many others, I was not given any help to face the parts I had ignored. Although my spiritual life was good, it had no anchor in my soul (remember, our soul is the seat of our intellect, will, and emotions). I could float around with great insights, but my life didn't change very much in the areas that mattered in day-to-day living. I knew a lot, but actually experienced little real peace and harmony within or without.

Survival Systems are what we use to hide ourselves in, often becoming our "idols." We tend to think of an idol as something in the Old Testament made of wood or stone, but idols are anything we put our trust in instead of, or above, God. Anything that we look to for life or hide ourselves in can be an idol. Our idols numb us by covering the real pain in our hearts and provide a false image that we sometimes believe is the real us. Being hidden with Christ in God is the only safe hiding place (Colossians 3:3,4).

Survival systems go all the way back to Adam and Eve in the Garden and the legitimate shame they experienced because of their sin. Instead of owning their sin and shame before God, they chose to try to cover and hide themselves with fig leaves. Just as fig leaves were used to cover their real shame, our systems can function in much the same way, covering the false shame of our deep-seated belief that we don't measure up. What is it we believe we're not enough for? It could be the standards others have placed on us for achievement or someone else's unrealistic expectations that were put on us. The pressure we feel to perform could come from the shame of our parents as they subtly demanded we fulfill the desires they couldn't attain for themselves. As you can see, it might not be any legitimate shame of our own that we're hiding, but the illegitimate or false shame that belongs to someone else. How many times on the little league field do we see a father demand his child come through so the father doesn't feel humiliated? Humiliation and embarrassment are both a form of shame. Instead of the game being fun for the child, he is robbed of his pleasure because in reality it is all about the father looking good in the eyes of others and perhaps achieving his unfulfilled dreams.

Our survival systems might also hide our fear of loss or shame, our disappointed longings, our feelings of emptiness, our fears of feeling overwhelmed and powerless or our struggles with feeling of out of control, as well as other emotions too numerous to mention. Our systems often begin early in childhood, but we perfect them over the years. When we were children, we thought like children and reasoned like children, but as adults we need to put away childish ways, as 1 Corinthians 13:11 reminds us. Those systems helped us make it through the difficult times as children, helped us survive, but now it's time to let them go and trust God with our identities instead of our created systems.

One woman I know who is allowing God to heal and restore her broken heart, began to recognize over 80 survival systems she had developed through the years so that when one didn't work another would take over. There were layers of systems so when one was seen and released, the next one would be revealed. They included things like performing perfectly, being an excellent server, avoiding real issues by rabbit-trailing, using anger to cover disappointed longings, food to hide in and bring comfort, sleep as an escape, self-contempt to cover feelings of shame, and on and on. Most of us don't have just one; there can be many systems that we cover ourselves with, yet far too often we don't recognize them as hiding places. Just like Adam and Eve after the fall, those systems are the *fig leaves* we use to cover our shame. Though their shame was legitimate, ours often come from the lie we have believed about ourselves that we're not enough just as we are (Genesis 3:7). Because of Jesus' finished work, we are already accepted just as we are!

The Bible tells us that "we have made a lie our refuge and falsehood our hiding place," but then it goes on to tell us that God will use circumstances to sweep away "our refuge, the lie" (Isaiah 28). For example, we might find ourselves in a circumstance where our usual survival system doesn't seem to be working. Perhaps we've used our performance in a job to give us worth, but then, because of the economy or some other situation, we lose that job and are unable to find another. Where is our worth then? Maybe we gained our identity from being a good mother and have hidden ourselves in our children, but one of them becomes rebellious and uncontrollable, bringing shame to the family. What feelings does a circumstance like that provoke within us? The Bible speaks of God shaking everything that can be shaken (Hebrews 12:27). It speaks of His shaking the "created things," so that "what cannot be shaken may remain."

Many are going through a tremendous shaking in their lives right now. The shaking might be in the area of their job, relationships, ministry, or in some other area. What is that all about? If we are to come to a place of true security in God, the things He must shake are the systems we have created to find our life. When that shaking comes, we often experience terror because it feels like we're being destroyed. It feels like that because the systems we've created have been so much a part of us and the false identity we developed, but that's a lie, they are not the real us.

We originally created those systems to prove ourselves acceptable and to hide the parts we deemed unacceptable from others' eyes. When those old false systems of ours finally get shaken loose, a new identity is able to be built on the firm foundation of Jesus Christ and the security and worth that can be found only in Him. God saw us before the foundation of the world and valued us before we were flesh and blood. He knew us before our parents did and called us forth from the womb. We are uniquely and wonderfully made because we are His creative masterpiece, made in His image and likeness (Psalm 139:14, Genesis 1:27). We were created on purpose and for purpose, but our own created systems will prevent the discovery of who we are truly meant to be since they are a false identity. Truth cannot be put on top of a lie and be expected to remain. We might be able to hold it for a short while, but it never lasts. Instead, our systems must be faced as the lies they are and released with a new trust in God that He is enough to cover us. Then we must come to a place of forgiveness for those who failed us. When all that occurs, the foundation of our lives can be rebuilt God's way with the truth of His word remaining without much effort at all, just with our agreement with God instead of the enemy. He then can begin to rebuild us on His new foundation of truth as we cooperate. "Unless the Lord builds the house, its builders labor in vain" (Psalm 127:1). We are that house that needs rebuilding.

A system of survival is a lie; it's an illusion that we have to keep propped up for fear of being found out. However, if our fear comes out of the illegitimate shame lie that says we're not enough just as we are, but only when we're performing well, we will use our system to keep the lie hidden. The system then becomes a false god that we serve, an idol that cannot save us, especially when our circumstances don't cooperate. Jesus came to set us free, to open the prison doors, but a false hiding place is bondage. He came to give us life that is really life, but a survival system takes our life instead of releasing it, driving us relentlessly to perform. Whatever we build we have to maintain, which takes an incredible amount of energy. God loves us too much and His plans for us are too great for Him to leave us there.

We have a multitude of systems to choose from: busyness, avoidance, blame, anger (revealed through verbal attacks when we feel threatened), the accumulation of things or people, performance, perfectionism or never trying very hard at anything. However, the purpose is to cover our fears, our emptiness, and our core shame belief of not feeling like we're enough without these systems. We might find ourselves trying to use the system of control with people, with our circumstances or with life itself because of being afraid to feel helpless or powerless. Although we might not be in touch with it, buried deep within there is often a fear of everything falling apart.

For many of us in childhood, things did fall apart and we have been trying ever since to never experience that frightening, out-of-control feeling again. We try to line up our ducks in a row or perform in a way that keeps everything safe, but then God allows all of our ducks to be shot! Of course our control is an illusion because, in reality, we can't hold our world together at all. Sadly, the more people don't cooperate with our agendas, or God doesn't cooperate, the harder we try to control. We then become even more desperate because of the terror that is lurking underneath and the feelings of powerlessness that are beginning to surface. A clue to our feeling out of control with the big issues can be revealed when we find ourselves trying to control the small insignificant things.

Sometimes a woman, when struggling with important relationships she can't control, will try to compulsively get her house, her appearance, and all else in perfect order, getting angry when others don't cooperate with her agenda. One man I knew felt undone because of his retirement. In his desperation to find something to control, he lined up his wife's spices in alphabetical order and demanded she keep them that way. The stability of our world comes from God not from us. "He is before all things, and in him all things hold together" (Colossians 1:17). He "sustains all things by his powerful word" (Hebrews 1:3). So it's safe to finally let go!

The systems mask the longings we're often not even in touch with, the desires and longings that are buried deep within. Our longings are to be accepted, enjoyed, valued, to be known as we are and still wanted. The systems are our coverings, the fig leaves we hide behind to present to the world around us. They're not us; they are merely an image. They cover over the unhealed pain we have experienced and the thwarted desires of the past, but they also prevent the very freedom we long for. They hide our true hearts and bury the person we have been created to be. No one really knows us when we hide ourselves because we can't really love or connect with a system even though we might receive admiration from afar. You can only truly love a person who allows their heart to be seen and connected with.

Several women come to mind that had hidden their hearts behind a tough-girl mask. Each of them was very efficient, intelligent, and capable, but until the coverings came off their hearts, they were impossible to connect with in any real way. I wanted to enjoy them, but couldn't because their heart was covered, their real self protected. I've never met a vulnerable heart I didn't love even with all its flaws, but it's the image, the system we've used that is so distasteful. It's a lonely, stressful life behind the system; it's a life of pretense and illusion, always waiting to be found out and discarded. That life of pretense will cause us to strive continually because we cannot afford to let down our guard and rest.

The scriptures tell us that God doesn't see as we see, but that He looks at the intents and motivations of the heart (1 Samuel 16:7). To quote John Eldredge in *Waking the Dead*, "A person's character is determined by his motives, and motive is always a matter of the heart." It's to the heart God desires to bring healing because by living in this broken world our hearts have been broken, sometimes without our even knowing it. Why have we chosen to cover the wonderful creation that we are?

The answer usually lies in some painful things that have happened to us along the journey of our lives. Those hurtful feelings have been buried away from our sight (and we hope from the sight of others), but continue to drive and motivate us on a deep heart level.

God desires us to be free to enjoy life and others, live for His glory, and care for His creation, which includes ourselves. He desires the gifts and talents He has put within us to be released to the world around us, whether in our home, our job, the neighborhood, marketplace, in church or wherever we happen to be. We simply overflow with the life that He is within us. Then, as the scriptures remind us, out of our innermost being will flow rivers of living water (John 7:38).

The wonderful thing is that my life will never look like yours or yours like anyone else's, but instead the flow will always come through the life of Christ manifesting in our own uniqueness. We each have a "piece" to bring, none of us is the whole "pie," but our pieces fit together to make that pie! To truly live life, we do it as a co-labor with God for His glory; not to have to prove ourselves or to try to get other people's acknowledgement or approval. We are already accepted as we are, even though we all come short of His glory (Romans 3:23).

When we know this on a heart level, we never have to worry about having to pretend because of the fear of being found out. God knows and sees us - the good, bad, and ugly - yet still receives us and desires to transform us from the inside out into His likeness that will be reflected through our own uniqueness!

Questions to Ponder

What motivates you to do the things you do?

Is there anything driving you so much that you don't feel free to rest?

Is there anything about yourself you are trying to hide and refuse to accept?

If you struggle with being a super-achiever, a pleaser, a performer, or a perfectionist, what do you get from it?

If you have a strong desire to have authority figures recognize and accept you, where might that have come from in your past?

If you feel driven to excel, whether it be at work, in raising your children, in sports, games or in any other endeavor you undertake, what do you get from it?
(Please note: excellence is important when our motivation is to truly co-labor with God for His glory, but it's important for us to discover the motivations of our hearts.)

Is your appearance extremely important to you, or perhaps the opposite, you don't seem to care about taking care of yourself, your home, or your possession at all? Why?

What do you want your home, auto or career to say about you?

Do you do things to impress others? Why?

Do you find yourself living by the world's demands instead of from your innermost being where God dwells? Why?

Assignment

Every time you feel you are messing up and falling short, at that moment, thank God that He loves you right now just the way you are.

Scriptures

"...First clean the inside of the cup and dish, and then the outside also will be clean." Matthew 23:26

"And we, who with unveiled faces all reflect the Lord's glory, are being transformed into His likeness with ever-increasing glory, which comes from the Lord, who is the Spirit." 2 Corinthians 3:18

9
CO-LABORING WITH JESUS

The Healing Process: Recap, Forgiveness, Helps for Healing, Recognizing Negative Emotions, Grieving Disappointed Longings, Enjoying Positive Emotions, The Exchange Process with Jesus, Receiving God's Truth

"For I, the Lord your God, will hold your right hand, saying to you, 'Fear not, I will help you." Isaiah 41:13

If you are anything like me, you will want your healing to come quickly. For that reason alone, it can be difficult to accept that healing is usually not an event, but a process. There will be significant events along the way and, after a major one occurs, it's easy to believe we're finished because of feeling so much freedom in that particular area. Sometimes God gives us a time of reprieve after one such healing, but then if we remain open, before long we will see there is more ground yet to be taken.

Giving God an open invitation to put the axe to any twisted roots that are affecting our lives and allowing Him to remain in charge while we stay in touch with the process opens the way to more areas of healing. Our job is to stay alert, with the Spirit's help, to any significant overreactions we might be having, especially when they happen several times in a row. Those overreactions can come from unhealed places or false beliefs within us. To begin the process of recognizing them and getting to the root, ask the Lord to help you see what the emotion is that you might be feeling. What age did you feel or sound like in your reaction? Did you sound more like a 3-year-old? Did you feel then like you are feeling in this overreaction? That can be a clue as to when the original wounding occurred. What happened? How were you hurt?

Also being aware of any significant dreams and the emotions you experienced in them can give helpful insight into what the Spirit might want to reveal to you. When hurt occurs, we often choose denial to distance and avoid them because we don't know what to do with the painful feelings. In that case, it will take the Spirit to bring revelation to break our denial. "Who can discern his errors? Forgive my hidden faults. Keep your servant also from willful sins; may they not rule over me…" (Psalm 19:12,13). Those unhealed places in us will rule over us and often cause us to sin by wounding others even though that's not our intention.

We all desire that things work well for us whether in our relationships, our work, our ministry or in any other life experiences. However, an honest look reveals seasons when things don't always go the way we think we need them to. Those are the times we often find ourselves depressed, resentful, avoiding, maybe even angry at God, whether we are willing to admit it or not. If you find yourself triggered or set-up several times with a similar emotion in a short time period, chances are God is after a particular wound He wants to heal even though the circumstances might look different. If you are usually a very logical and analytical person and instead find yourself emotionally reacting, that can be a clue to ask God to show you where the emotions might be coming from.

I've discovered that God often triggers me in sets of three. In a period of a few days, I might find myself overreacting in several different situations. Since this is not the norm, I'll ask the Spirit to show me what I was feeling in each occurrence. If the *emotion* appears to be similar in every circumstance, even though the *situations* are different, I know He's after something. It's a clue for me to identify what the emotion was and then ask Him to reveal the original wound or false belief that carried those same feelings.

Often, an old memory will surface from the past, one I had totally forgotten about or thought was insignificant. My first step toward healing is to connect the emotion I'm currently feeling with that particular memory and allow Jesus to meet me there. Next is to move toward forgiving whoever hurt me from my heart and release them from my judgment. Notice I said, "move toward," because coming to total forgiveness can be a process. One man I helped found himself overreacting with anger whenever anyone innocently questioned him about something. Since his overreaction happened so frequently, he began to see his reaction might be coming from something in the past. As we explored with the Spirit's help, we found that as a child he had been often falsely accused and blamed for the actions of his sibling. As he saw that and forgave his sister, healing came.

When we are willing to continue to allow the Spirit to work this way, many such healings can take place, freeing us up in the present to live and relate to others in a much healthier way. With each emotional healing, it's as if we begin to feel lighter, things become clearer, we feel more at peace, and our reactions and responses to others get healthier.

A Recap of the Healing Process in Co-labor with the Holy Spirit

Begin with prayer that comes from the heart and ask the Spirit to help you be alert to anything of significance that He wants to show you. "Search me O God, and know my heart; test me and know my anxious thoughts. See if there is any offensive way in me, and lead me in the way everlasting." (Psalm 139:23,24)

Pay attention to any set-ups or your emotional overreactions in present situations. Ask: "What am I feeling right now?" Name the emotion. You will find a helpful list of emotions later on in this chapter. Ask: "When did I feel this way before?" It might come from an unresolved situation in the not-too-distant past or go all the way back to childhood.

Include God in the process: "God, please show me where this comes from so I can be healed from the past situation as well as from the present one."

Be alert to any memories that might fleetingly surface. They might come from any age, child to adult, or perhaps a person's name might come to mind. "God, is there a wound You want me to pay attention to?" If the memory goes back to childhood, ask yourself if there is a hurt little child within that needs to be embraced and brought to Jesus for healing?

Remember how Jesus is pictured in the Bible, tenderly inviting the little children to come to Him for blessing (Matthew 19:13). Jesus is fiercely protective of the little children (Luke 17:1-3).

If God does allow an old memory to surface, pay attention to the feelings you felt in the original circumstance. If God brought a person's name to mind, ask Him if there is an unhealed wound connected to that person. What were the feelings? "How old was I?" If it goes way back to age 9, it can be the 9-year-old stuck within that needs the healing, not necessarily your adult self. Remember that Jesus is outside of time and is able to go back into your past as well as into your future (Hebrews 13:8). Feel your feelings. "Jesus, please meet me in those painful feelings and, since you suffered with similar emotions, help me to make the exchange with you of my hurtful emotions for your peace." (Isaiah 53:1-5 and Hebrews 2:17-18)

Then begin moving toward forgiveness: "God, please help me to release forgiveness from my heart to the one who has hurt me in the past as well the one as in the present situation. I can't do this by myself, so I join with You in Your forgiveness for that person. I release my judgment toward them and give over the power of judgment to You alone. Thanks." Agreeing with Jesus, we say, "Father, forgive them, for they do not know what they are doing" (Luke 23:34).

Forgiveness

Sometimes being able to forgive from the heart can be a lengthy process, but keep moving toward it, no matter how long it takes you. Forgiveness is for you; it sets you free. When forgiving someone, you are releasing that person to God so you are freed from carrying the burden of their offense. Judgment then becomes God's and He is the only one who is able to see all things and judge rightly. Vengeance is His alone.

We are meant to be people of light, free to walk in the light as He is in the light. Holding onto our unforgiveness creates darkness within us by covering our heart and affects our relationship with God (1 John 1:5-7). Coming to the place of forgiving from the heart, as the scriptures ask us to, can be very difficult. We can often get to a place of forgiveness in our minds, but if it never reaches our hearts, the offended feelings will continually return.

The process can be helped along by praying blessings over that person every time they come to mind, turning them over to God again and again. It might take a while for the forgiveness to get to the heart, but we will feel free when it's finally completed. My first true heart forgiveness took several months before I was finally able to let go of my anger so I could fully release that person to God. He was a very significant person in my early life and the wound went very deep. As a result, my anger had become a fortress of self-protection that covered my wounded heart.

Since it was the heart that was wounded, it's our heart God desires to heal. However, we can't release what we have buried and not allowed ourselves to feel. That's why facing or owning the emotion we felt is so important in order for us to finally be able to let it go. We can only surrender to God that which we know and have awareness of. God asks us to forgive the one who hurt us just as He has forgiven us. If we will allow Him, the Spirit (the Helper) will help us do what seems impossible. So join Him in moving toward it, but without condemnation, just a willing heart. Be patient if you find you can't get there as fast as you would like, just don't quit. Remember, it is God who works in us "to will and to act according to His good purpose" when we allow Him (Philippians 2:13).

In the same way, when we have deeply hurt others and then asked them to forgive us, we need to give them the space to allow God to heal their heart and work in them a willingness to forgive.

That time of waiting can be very difficult. I've watched many parents who have unintentionally wounded their children out of their own unhealed areas and, even though they've confessed to their children and asked for forgiveness, it has taken the children time to finally release their anger and forgive.

Excusing someone is not forgiving them, it is simply sweeping the offense under the carpet at your own expense. Excusing is saying, "My wound doesn't matter, I'll just overlook it and let you go free." Instead, forgiveness says, "My wound does matter very much both to God and to me, but I'm choosing not to be your judge. I'm leaving that to God and releasing you from my judgment. I am setting me free by setting you free."

The other temptation we face is to minimize the offense so it doesn't feel so bad. This, too, is just sweeping our angry and painful emotions under the carpet. We must see things the way they are if we are to release them fully to God so that we are able to grieve whatever loss came out of the offense. Jesus is a forgiver and as He hung on the cross He cried out in His agony, "Father forgive them, for they know not what they are doing" (Luke 23:34). That was not minimizing or excusing, instead His forgiveness of us cost Him much pain, anguish, and His very blood. He never said His blood didn't matter, but He *chose* to shed it for us so we could be free.

We are unable to truly forgive from our heart without drawing on Jesus, the forgiver who lives inside of us. God is a God of light, but hidden resentment and unforgiveness within is darkness that silently invites the enemy to bring us torment. Jesus had no darkness in Him at all so Satan had no power over Him (John 14:30). "Anyone who claims to be in the light, but hates his brother is still in the darkness. Whoever loves his brother lives in the light, and there is nothing in him to make him stumble. But whoever hates his brother is in the darkness and walks around in the darkness; he does not know where he is going because the darkness has blinded him." (1 John 2:9-11) "Bear with each other and forgive whatever grievances you may have against one another. Forgive as the Lord forgave you." (Colossians 3:13)

Helps in the Healing Process

Journaling Journaling is invaluable as we begin our healing journey. Personally, I prefer to write letters to God instead of just writing in a journal. I hand write my letters to Him and use a pretty journal, but others prefer using the computer because they can type faster than they can write. In that process, instead of writing from your mind, allow yourself to express the feelings of your heart to God, both negative and positive. If a hurt occurred in your childhood, express the feelings of the wounded child. Sometimes it's not very pretty, but it will help to get in touch with what your heart was really feeling at that time. In writing to God, you are sharing your deepest emotions with Him, and inviting Him in on the process of helping you discover who He created you to be. This creates wonderful intimacy with Him, as well as brings healing to your emotions.

Since it is God who has always known us in all of our good, bad, and ugliness, who better to help us peel back the layers to get to the real issues that are locked within our hearts? Don't be afraid to ask God the questions you are struggling with in your heart, but just be willing to let Him bring forth any answers in His timing. The things He does not show you might remain a mystery to you until you finally see Him face-to-face. When I first began writing my letters to God over twenty years ago, I had more questions than anything else. In His timing He answered many of them, but not all. In writing to God, it's important to remember to share the feelings of your heart, not just the facts, if awareness and release are to come.

I have been writing to God daily for all these years and it has probably been the most valuable thing I have done. If circumstances prevent my letters from being written for more than three days, I find that I lose touch with my own heart. Keep in mind that it's through the heart we develop intimacy with God as well as maintain connection with ourselves and others. So through this simple exercise we begin to develop a journey toward deep soul intimacy with God, the one who knows everything there is to know about us - the good, bad, and ugly - and who still loves, accepts and enjoys us. This then frees us to be more honest and transparent in our sharing with others as well. "Therefore confess your sins to each other and pray for each other so that you may be healed" (James 5:16).

As mentioned previously, writing a letter that is never going to be sent to anyone who has deeply hurt us is also a helpful tool in working through our feelings. That can help us come to healing and then enable us to release forgiveness toward them. If our wound occurred in childhood, write the letter for the child who has been buried within. Listen to that little one's feelings and express them on paper.

A Thankful Heart An important key to maintaining health is to develop a thankful heart. As you look back at the hurtful, negative realities, the enemy will attempt to consume you with them. Though those losses must be grieved and not minimized, there are little gifts every day we can rejoice over at the same time. Without grieving the losses, we will tend to overlook the gifts because they might seem so insignificant. They are not! As we learn to receive those gifts, our hearts can feel joy in the midst of our sorrow.

We have all been through a period when everything seemed to break and had to be replaced at significant cost. The dollar signs were definitely marching out the door! When you're on a fixed income, you notice those things, but we all know the disappointment of just waiting for another shoe to drop. As my losses continued to go on, I became discouraged about it all. However, my eyes also began to be opened to see so many little blessings that meant even more than they would have had I not faced my disappointments. There were wonderful gifts. Things like a friend who willingly came over to help with some technology I felt quite helpless in dealing with. There was a wonderful meal at a place we weren't usually able to enjoy. There was a repairman who replaced something free of charge. There was a sweet, appreciative email from someone who had moved away.

Be aware of the little things you might have just regarded as your due or ignored because they weren't important enough and give thanks! It is necessary to see that life is not all good or all bad, but each day has mixture. We must give up any unrealistic expectations we might have placed on things or people. They, as well as ourselves, are a mixture! Each morning in my letter to God, I list the things I'm thankful for from the day before. I know it encourages His heart as it does mine!

Discovering God in His Creation "The heavens declare the glory of God; the skies proclaim the work of His hands" (Psalm 19:1). Another way we can co-labor with the Spirit toward restoration is to spend time in God's wonderful creation. Sometimes this can be more soothing in a healing season than being in a more spiritual setting. There is a reflection of God in His creation that expresses wonder and peace in a way that can restore our souls. By listening to our hearts, we can become aware of the particular part of nature that seems to draw us to sooth our struggling heart.

Not too many years ago, during a difficult season, I remember being on vacation at the river of my childhood in Pennsylvania. I had a little blow-up boat that I tied to a tree and anchored in the cool shade. As I rested there, I listened to the gentle flow of the river all around me and watched the shadows dance. In that peaceful setting of God's wonderful creation, I could sense the restoring of my weary soul. What draws you? Is it being on the beach and listening to the crashing of the ocean waves, sitting on a rock by a quiet stream, watching a glorious sunrise or sunset, taking a quiet walk in the woods, enjoying the shapes and movement of puffy white clouds or doing some other thing that warmly reminds you of your childhood? Responding to the call of God's creation feeds a part of us that is usually ignored and forgotten. Wonder is a need that must be acknowledged and fed for it connects us to the God who is bigger than our problems.

For me, there is nothing I love more than tubing peacefully on that lazy river though I'm only able to do that occasionally. Just regularly taking time to be outside in God's wonderful creation feeds and restores my soul and, because water is very soothing to me, when it's not possible to be outside, simply standing in the running water of the shower can be restorative as well.

Regaining Our Trust "Do not let your hearts be troubled. Trust in God, trust also in Me." (John 14:1) Trust in God is necessary if we are to come through our wounded emotions to a place of peace. However, because trust has so often been betrayed in our lives and we frequently have the fear of being betrayed again, we can be afraid to trust God very deeply or to trust people again at the heart level. Perhaps the opposite might be true for you and you find yourself trusting people foolishly. To open our hearts to trust once more in a healthy way requires that we face the pain of our hurts and forgive those who have wounded us. We are to value one another and ourselves as God's precious creation, honoring Him by loving each other, but always with realistic expectations. There are times when we all disappoint and hurt one another even when it's not our intention. The scriptures remind us that we will all come short of His glory, that none of us is perfect (Romans 3:23). However, when we are unable to value and accept either ourselves or one another, it's a sign there are still places in our hearts to be restored.

Learning to trust after being betrayed is a difficult journey that requires the risk of opening our hearts again. I know how difficult it has been for me to learn to set out into the deep and not just hug the shore. Without being aware of it, I had made a silent vow after my own abuse that I'd never trust again, that I would stay on the alert and be hyper-vigilant at all times, always protecting my heart. The problem is that it's lonely inside our fortresses and we can't have real relationships that way. Vows like that must be broken. To make matters worse, we were created as relational beings, but in order to have healthy relationships, our first relational trust must always be with God. Jesus reveals that His trust was not foolishly in man, but that He was trusting God with His life. "But Jesus would not entrust Himself to them, for He knew all men" (John 2:24). When we are willing to trust God, not that we'll never be hurt, but that at our core we will not be destroyed by it, we can begin to let go of our self-protection and relate to others from the heart, all the while entrusting our lives to Him. Remember that the opposite of love is not hate, but self-protection.

UNDERSTANDING THE PROCESS

Seasons "There is a time for everything, and a season for every activity under heaven" (Ecclesiastes 3:1-8). We must understand that, just as in nature, our life in God has seasons. The wonderful thing about seasons is that they change. No season lasts forever. The enemy may whisper to us, especially when we are in a dark season, that things will never change, but we must recognize that as the lie it is. There are times of experiencing a winter season when all seems dead and dry. However, just like with nature, that season also has purpose. If we will not get angry and bitter, God can do much internal work in us during that time. Just as in a northern winter, when it appears that nothing is happening and all seems dead, there is much going on beneath the surface that we can't see. I'm always amazed at the new life that comes forth in a person after their winter is over and their spring season begins. Just as it happens at the end of a cold winter in nature, the beginning of spring is almost imperceptible. If we will remain patient, the flowers slowly begin to bloom again and the grass eventually comes forth lush and green.

I can remember the exact moment when, at the end of my own long winter season, I heard the gentle voice of God saying to my hungry heart, "It's time to plant the flowers again." Yet even though my spring season began early that morning as I was driving to breakfast in the dark, it was some time before I could actually see the flowers begin to bloom.

Another way of describing the winter season could be similar to going through a wilderness or desert experience. It's like our life gets a "time-out" when nothing works as it did before. It can be a dark, confusing time if we don't understand that it is a season when God is working deep within us. I went through a long wilderness season in which God did many wonderful things that I didn't recognize until afterward. Although the wilderness season was long, there was a three-month period within it that was very dark. At that time, it was like God was no longer there. I couldn't hear Him or sense His presence and even my Bible seemed closed to me. He gave me one wonderful verse, however, to sustain me. "I will give you the treasures of darkness, riches stored in secret places, that you may know that I am the Lord...who summons you by name" (Isaiah 45:3). It was in that darkness that I learned to trust Him.

One young man I counseled had a definite call of God on his life and, prior to the desert season, he had been used in a mighty way. Then, for no reason he could understand, it seemed like everything stopped. He prayed and prayed and the heavens seemed like brass. On top of that, everything seemed to go wrong causing him to feel powerless and forsaken by God. He began to struggle angrily with God in greater measure than he had ever allowed himself before since he felt so abandoned. At the time, this young man had no understanding that this was a season God was allowing in order to bring forth even greater preparation in his life for his part in building God's kingdom.

Just as Israel (and even Jesus) spent time in the wilderness, we sometimes go through a similar experience. Because it's a time when nothing seems to work for us and doors that formerly opened wide are closed, it can be a time of feeling disoriented in our walk with God. The wilderness season often raises more questions than it answers, but it's a good time to ask the questions even though we might hear nothing in return. In due time, we will understand all that God has accomplished in us through that season. It's also a time when God tears down some of our systems because they no longer seem to work as they once did. The Bible gives a clue as to the purpose of that wilderness season for the nation of Israel. "Remember how the Lord your God led you all the way in the desert … to humble you and to test you in order to know what was in your heart, whether or not you would keep His commands" (Deuteronomy 8:7). It's a time of our learning to trust God in spite of the apparent lack of His blessing. It is there that we often begin to recognize our hunger and seek the food that really satisfies our hearts. We have a beautiful truth pictured in Song of Songs 8:5, "Who is this coming up from the desert leaning on her lover?" Our lover of course, is Jesus. We go into the desert independent, self-confident, and full of our own agendas. We come out *leaning*, dependent and confident in Jesus alone, with His ways becoming our ways more and more, and finally understanding the truth that without Him we can do nothing (John 15:5).

The Healing of Our False Perceptions Jesus tells us, "Your eye is the lamp of your body. When your eyes are good, your whole body also is full of light. But when they are bad, your body also is full of darkness. See to it, then, that the light within you is not darkness. Therefore, if your whole body is full of light, and no part of it dark, it will be completely lighted, as when the light of a lamp shines on you." (Luke 11:34-36) Our eyes have to do with our perceptions, our paradigms, and how we view life. When we have false perceptions that have come out of painful circumstances, those perceptions can cause pain that can affect our lives on a daily basis. From our perceptions, we often develop paradigms that are false. A paradigm is a way of seeing or the model of life we have that might or might not necessarily be true. Our perceptions and paradigms cause us to interpret life, but our truth might not be factual truth.

In 1990, a year with a number of difficult circumstances happening in my life all at once, a huge paradigm shift had to take place within me. Through some false teaching, I believed that God should not allow suffering or, if He did, He should fix it quickly. It took almost the entire year, but as a result of having to deeply struggle with who God really is, my whole way of seeing was shifted. That resulted in a new-found peace and intimacy with God, as well as a fresh understanding of the Scriptures. I had to finally accept the fact that I might not always understand His ways because, as the scripture tells us, they are "higher than ours" (Isaiah 55:8,9).

One false perception I developed came from the pain of growing up in an emotionally disconnected family. Because I continually experienced feeling lonely and isolated, my perception caused me to believe I was unloved, unaccepted, and there was something wrong with me. Although that was my truth, it wasn't factual truth and it created darkness within me. After finally crying out to God for healing, He surfaced the pain, but also began to reveal His truth to me. God desires that we have "truth in our inner being" (our hearts) and not just in our heads alone (Psalm 51). The truth I had to accept in my heart was that my family was incapable of loving me the way I longed to be loved because of their own unhealed wounds, yet they still loved me even though I was unable to experience it at the time. After receiving this revelation, it was necessary for me to begin to forgive them from my heart and not just excuse them.

How we perceive reality also comes out in our interactions with other people. So many times I hear someone interpret another's response to them as rejection, when in reality the person was just having a bad day themselves. One woman, April, left a message on her friend's voice mail, but a few days went by and the friend didn't return her phone call. April got angry and felt rejected. Later that week, she was embarrassed to hear that her friend was going through a major crisis in her own life and was overwhelmed with her own problems. April realized the hard way that her friend's lack of response had nothing to do with her at all! False perceptions cause us to put ourselves in the center of our universe instead of allowing others to have their own struggles too.

Any false perception we have will rob our peace and throw us into pain, anxiety or perhaps control. It can cause us to explode with anger and react in all sorts of negative ways. For example, if we have the perception that life is supposed to be fair then whenever we experience injustice we will overreact with anger. The truth is that Jesus was not treated fairly even though He was perfect and He assures us that as He was persecuted and unfairly treated, we would be also (John 15:20). That's another reminder that we do not live in the Garden, but in a broken world. One day, Jesus assures us, He will return and finally set things right and the life we have always longed for will finally be a reality.

God's Holy Housecleaning We are in a time of God's holy housecleaning. There are places within all of us where the doors have been locked on rooms that have been filled with old hurts, offenses, resentments, and debris from the past. Outside of those rooms, the floors are swept and the junk is thrown out, but every once in a while, something happens to us that causes the debris from behind the locked doors to be disturbed. I don't know about you, but I desire to have light flow throughout my soul. I don't want any hidden rooms with doors that I have to worry about keeping locked. It takes energy to keep them closed and along with that is the lurking fear of the hidden things someday being exposed.

Recently, someone who has begun the process of healing from their painful childhood abuse, shared with me they are just now seeing the energy they have expended in trying to bury that horrific pain. God is a God of light, life, and liberty so we are meant to be people of the same without any secrets or hidden darkness that allow the enemy, who is darkness himself, to bring us into fear and torment.

The Progressive Journey of Healing One of the statements I hear all the time is, "I've already dealt with that so I'm finished." Believing this can be the enemy's tactic to get us to give up the progressive journey of healing. Remember, we're often like an onion with layer after layer needing to be peeled back.

There was a time when, years after receiving healing and forgiving my father, a situation triggered some buried pain I had not connected with before. For most of my life I struggled with the lie that whenever something I enjoyed ended nothing good would ever be there to replace it. This caused me to fear letting go and trusting that God was good. In revealing the lie I had believed, God allowed me to remember how my father would take things away, but usually give nothing back to replace it. That caused me to fear loss. After inviting Jesus to meet me there with His healing, I was able to forgive my father for that as well and freedom was quickly enjoyed. It took only moments, but it set me free in a crucial area that I had struggled with for years! In some measure, I believe I will be on this journey with Jesus in the restoring of my soul until my healing is finally complete by seeing Him face-to-face. The Bible reminds us, "But we know that when He appears, we shall be like Him, for we shall see Him as He is" (1 John 3:2). In the meantime, "we are being transformed into His likeness with ever-increasing glory" (2 Corinthians 3:18).

There are things within us that we can remain unaware of until they are triggered in the present. When people are not in close relationship, it often appears they are fine, but that's only because nothing buried within is being triggered. We tend to be sandpaper for each other, which can be a good thing if it brings us to healing. Unfortunately though, when triggered we usually just get hurt, angry or blame the person who triggered us.

Even after major roots have been removed, God desires to fine-tune the motivations of our hearts, using an even finer grade of sandpaper, but He needs our cooperation to do so. Jesus has already done His part for our freedom, but it doesn't become ours until we join with Him on our own behalf receiving healing, restoration, and the releasing of freedom by forgiving the ones who have hurt us.

Generational Healing When we cooperate with Jesus for our own healing, He can then use us as wounded healers on behalf of others as well. It usually takes one person to begin the emotional healing process that can eventually bring change to an entire family. That makes a way for the curses of many generations to be turned to blessings for ourselves and for future generations. It is important to note that we can't change others, but as we begin to allow change in ourselves, others often change the way they relate to us because the old games that were played no longer work. It takes two to play a game so when one quits the game is over.

One person in a family allowing change can make a way for the rebuilding and restoration to begin. "They will rebuild the ancient ruins and restore the places long devastated; they will renew the ruined cities that have been devastated for generations" (Isaiah 61:4).

What do emotions look like? How do I know what I'm feeling?

So many people have buried their feelings to the point that they no longer recognize what an emotion is. They get their thoughts and feelings mixed up by saying, "I think" when they mean, "I feel" or vice versa. Below you will find a list of emotions to help you identify what it is you might be feeling. Remember, our feelings were given to us for a purpose, revealing what our hearts are struggling with so we can cooperate with God in taking any action necessary for healing. Our emotions must be identified so we can get beyond them and not remain stuck. If we don't know when we are sad or disappointed we can't grieve the disappointment, move toward forgiveness, and get on with our lives in a healthy way.

Without owning it, the feeling will often get buried within causing resentment to build. When this happens, the overflow of our hearts usually comes out wrongly in contempt, blame or a wrong attitude. We will begin to shut down inside, closing our hearts either toward God, the one who caused our disappointment, or ourselves on the deepest level. Identifying our emotions is like the map we find at the entrance to the mall, "You Are Here." By locating ourselves in our feelings, we can then take the appropriate action toward healing and release.

Recognizing Negative Emotions

Expressions of Anger Feelings of anger could come out in emotions such as hate, resentment, criticism, judgment, disappointment, contempt, sarcasm, frustration, hostility, irritation, jealousy, envy, bitterness, depression, skepticism, selfishness or feeling distant or bored. We might be trying to cover our feelings of shame or powerlessness by using anger or rage.

Anger, being a covering emotion, usually makes us feel powerful when deep down inside we are feeling very powerless, helpless, shamed or trapped. When identifying what we are feeling, we don't want to stop with the emotion of anger, but seek with the help of God's Spirit to find out what is underneath it. Often there are feelings of fear, shame, and hurt of some kind, a loss or the emotion of powerlessness hidden beneath.

Anger, when faced and worked through in a healthy way, gives us new boldness and courage. We are supposed to be angry at what God is angry at, like robbery. "I hate robbery and iniquity" (Isaiah 61:8). Jesus cleaned the temple with great anger and courage, knowing He would experience the wrath of the religious leaders of His day. He said, "My house will be called a house of prayer, but you are making it a den of robbers" (Matthew 21:12,13). If we are to stand with Him for the things He stands for, we must work through the unhealthy anger that comes from being wounded. Becoming who we were created to be requires a willingness to join God in the fight for our life and, just as He does, anger at the thief (Satan) who came to steal, kill, and destroy you (John 10:10).

"In your anger do not sin. Do not let the sun go down while you are still angry." (Ephesians 4:26) "In your anger do not sin; when you are on your beds, search your hearts and be silent" (Psalm 4:4). In other words, anger is a valid emotion, but it must be worked through to be released in a healthy way. Facing our anger is usually followed by the need to forgive the source of our anger.

Expressions of Fear Feelings of fear could manifest as insecurity, insignificance, anxiety, nervousness, powerlessness, helplessness, feeling overwhelmed, undone, overlooked, insecure, jealous, envious, discouraged, confused, rejected, discarded, dismissed, embarrassed, shamed, rejected or abandoned. Fear drives the need to remain in control.

When you discover you have feelings of fear, invite the Spirit's help to finish these sentences: "I am afraid because _____," or "I am afraid of _____." We can only surrender to God that which we know, so we must get our fears into the light if we are to release them.

Fear must be faced. If we bury or run from it, it will pursue us and grow even larger. I've known people who allowed their fears to get so big they were afraid to leave home, living in torment of going out in public. Sadly, one woman didn't leave her house for several years. As she allowed her fears to dictate and rule her, the world she lived in became smaller and smaller and fear began to consume her freedom. It was a great battle to regain her life since the fear had gotten such a foothold, but she finally made it. It is much better to face any fear we might be struggling with early on.

"Be strong and courageous. Do not be afraid or terrified because of them, for the Lord your God goes with you; He will never leave you or forsake you." (Deuteronomy 31:6) "I have chosen you and have not rejected you. So do not fear, for I am with you; do not be dismayed for I am your God. I will strengthen you and help you; I will uphold you with my righteous right hand." (Isaiah 41:9,10)

Take the hand of Jesus and walk into whatever you might be afraid of, but this time you are not alone, for He goes with you and His promise is that, "When you pass through the waters, I will be with you; and when you pass through the rivers, they will not sweep over you. When you walk through the fire, you will not be burned; the flames will not set you ablaze. For I am the Lord your God, the Holy One of Israel, your Savior." (Isaiah 43:2,3)

Expressions of Shame Shame feelings could manifest as feeling guilty, inadequate, inferior, unworthy, unacceptable, never measuring up, unlovely, unattractive, and ugly or feeling like a failure. Shame could be covered over with contempt at either yourself in the form of self-hatred or at others in anger, judgment, criticism or sarcasm.

"Do not be afraid; you will not suffer shame. Do not fear disgrace; you will not be humiliated. You will forget the shame of your youth." (Isaiah 54:4)

Expressions of Sadness or Sorrow Sadness could reveal itself as confusion, apathy, loneliness, depression, feeling distracted, dissatisfied, bored, stupid, ashamed, disappointed, remorseful, unhappy, isolated, struggles with sleepiness, feelings of loss or wanting to cry unexpectedly. "…weeping may remain for a night, but rejoicing comes in the morning" (Psalm 30:5b).

Grieving Our Disappointed Longings

The grieving process is God's way to help us deal with the sorrows and losses of this broken world. We were born with longings for the Garden, but instead, we have all been wounded and disappointed many times over. Our pictures of what we thought our lives were supposed to look like have been broken. What do we do with all that disappointment? God's way is for us to grieve it. In the scriptures we see Israel calling for the wailing women to help them grieve, but in today's culture, we just try to get over our losses without fully acknowledging them. When we bury them, they are not worked through and will surface in one form or another at a later time. Of course, how long and difficult the grieving process is depends on the nature of our loss.

More than a year ago, my husband went through a time of difficult heart surgery with a number of complications that affected his COPD and his everyday life and health in various ways. We often have expectations that we should recover quickly and things should look the way they did before the crisis, however, sometimes the effects go on for a very long time. We did some grieving in the beginning, of course, but realized many months later we were not finished grieving over the many continued losses that both of us were still experiencing in different ways. As we once again recognized there was more disappointment to face, and therefore more grieving to be done, our hearts actually began to feel lighter instead of heavier.

Stages of Grief In the early stages of grief there is often shock. We might feel distracted or numb; try to deny our pain or bargain with God. At some point, we will usually feel anger, disappointment, and sorrow, which can sometimes come in alternating waves with short reprieves in between. When we allow ourselves to pass through all the emotions, as long as we don't get stuck indefinitely in denial or in one particular feeling, they will eventually diminish in intensity. In due time, we will pass through to the other side and find ourselves in a new place of peace and acceptance.

One woman I helped a while back lost her husband five years before we met. She had never allowed herself to grieve his death so she remained stuck in the denial of her pain. Through using busyness as an escape, she was able to function fairly well with tasks on the job, but remained stunted relationally and in other ways. As we opened up her unhealed grief, the dam burst open and she was finally able to go through the remaining stages of grief. Grief doesn't just go away, it must be processed to get all the way through. It will take as long as it takes, but there is a new day on the other side. Although she had a death to grieve, the same is true on perhaps a lesser scale for any loss we might have suffered.

When we have finally come to terms with our loss, joy can begin to replace our sorrow. Unlike happiness, which largely depends on the happenings around us, we can experience joy in spite of our sorrow (Psalm 30:5). The Bible refers to two different types of sorrow. There is a sorrow that eventually brings resurrection life to us or there is a worldly sorrow that paralyzes. Worldly sorrow can lead to self-pity and a victim mentality bringing no life with it at all, just ongoing disappointment.

Lost Hope When we go through a long season of disappointment and loss we can easily lose hope, especially when things do not change quickly and God doesn't seem to hear us. "Hope deferred makes the heart sick, but a longing fulfilled is a tree of life" (Proverbs 13:12). In that season, despair can begin to overwhelm us and we can feel hopeless because, without realizing it, we have put our hope in people, our circumstances changing, or in God acting in a certain way on our behalf. However, despair can actually become a "door of hope" because when our false hopes crumble, a new hope in God alone can begin to be birthed within us. (In Hosea 2:15, the valley of Achor, which means trouble, becomes a door of hope.) That hope knows nothing except the fact that God's heart toward us is good even though we have no idea as to how things will work out. The scriptures tell us that those who hope in Him will not be disappointed (Isaiah 49:23). This new hope is in Him alone and not in His blessings or in our picture of how He will act. These days, God is shaking everything that can be shaken and many are losing the false hopes they had put their faith in. However, as they enter the process, a new faith and hope in God alone begins to slowly emerge out of the darkness.

Enjoying Our Positive Emotions

When we shut down our negative feelings, we aren't free to experience the positive ones very deeply if at all. Our hearts have wonderful, positive emotions that we don't want to ignore or be unable to fully enjoy. For years I was dead inside, feeling numb because I had buried my negative feelings. Once my buried emotions were faced, healed, and those who hurt me were forgiven, I began to experience many positive emotions. I began to see life differently. All of life is a mixture, but we don't want it to be so. We often demand it be all good because we desperately want to live happily ever after. However, in a fallen world that is not possible. The saying, "It's all good," is often spoken glibly, but in reality it's not all good, it's mixed! We must grieve the sadness so we can fully enjoy that which is good. When we view life honestly, we see there are gifts and losses in each day. Grieving our losses opens the way to much more fully enjoying the gifts of each day, not just viewing things as all good or bad. We will begin to see God working in all things for our ultimate good even when we don't understand what He's doing (Ecclesiastes 7:14).

Expressions of Positive Emotions Some examples of positive emotions might be to feel hopeful, creative, cheerful, thankful, funny, free spirited, lighthearted, inspired, confident, faithful, discerning, valuable, appreciated, respected, worthwhile, trusting, relaxed, content, thoughtful, intimate, loving, secure, nurturing, caring, kind, adventurous, forgiven, and cared for. Two wonderful positive emotions we all long for are joy and peace that, in their truest form, can only come from the life of Christ in us.

Expressions of Joy Joyfulness can be hopeful, optimistic, creative, cheerful, energetic, stimulating, fascinating, daring, filled with anticipation, free spirited, light hearted, and encouraged. The wonderful thing about joy is that it doesn't depend on "happenings" or on what's going on around us; instead, it's felt deep within. We can even experience joy in sorrowful times because joy originates in God, is a fruit of the Spirit, and has it's hope in God, not in our circumstances. "But the fruit of the Spirit is love, joy, peace, patience, kindness, goodness, faithfulness, gentleness and self-control…" (Galations 5:22,23).

Expressions of Peace Peacefulness can be felt as contentment, thoughtfulness, responsiveness, restfulness, serenity, being relaxed, enjoying intimacy, feeling secure, trusting, nurturing, caring, and having kindness. True peace can only come from finding our security in God. That security comes from Christ in us and not from outside circumstances. Often, much effort is expended toward trying to obtain security from finances, relationships, our jobs, and other things the world offers, but all those can be lost and are not secure at all. The security from Christ in us is a solid Rock to build our lives on. He will never forsake us. He is not far off, but living right within us at all times. "Let the peace of Christ rule in your hearts…" (Colossians 3:15). "And the peace of God, which transcends all understanding, will guard your hearts and your minds in Christ Jesus" (Philippians 4:7).

Expressions of Powerful Feelings Powerful feelings could be experienced as confidence, faithfulness, helpfulness, being wisely able to trust, discerning, respectful of self and others, adventurous, self-assured, feeling worthwhile, valuable, appreciated, able to take wise risks, having courage and boldness, as well as numerous other emotions.

Powerful feelings in the truest sense come from God's power and His life within us. Christ's power is made perfect in our weakness (2 Corinthians 12:8-10). When we try to control others or our circumstances, we are using false power or an illusion of power to cover our fear and weakness. When we've been hurt in the past, we often try to avoid weakness feeling it's a bad thing, but the apostle Paul shared that he delighted in weakness so that Christ's power could rest on him (2 Corinthians 12:10). Paul states, "When I am weak, then I am strong," because that strength comes from Christ's power instead of his own. The Bible reminds us that Jesus had to be crucified in weakness so He could make the exchange with us of His power for our weakness (2 Corinthians 13:4).

Jesus Experienced Similar Emotions

Have you ever been disappointed by your friends when you needed them most? Because Jesus had to suffer in every way as we do in order to be able to make an exchange with us, His longings were also disappointed. Jesus was deeply distressed and troubled and said to His three closest friends, "Stay here and keep watch" (Mark 14:34). That was a heartfelt request to the ones closest to Him to remain alert with Him in His hardest hour. He longed for them to remain with Him and not leave Him alone in His pain, but instead of supporting Him, they fell asleep. Having that desire deeply disappointed, He asked them, "Are you … asleep? Could you not keep watch with me one hour?" (Mark 14:37) Because of His lonely struggle on the worst night of His life, He can certainly connect with you in your feelings of loneliness and isolation.

Have you ever been hurt and betrayed by those you trusted?

Jesus was betrayed by Judas and denied and deeply disappointed by Peter, one of His closest friends. "Before the rooster crows today you will deny three times that you know me" (Luke 22:34). After Jesus rose from the dead, Peter, who was feeling disqualified because of what he had done, went back to fishing. Then Jesus the Restorer singled Peter out and asked Peter three times if he loved Him (John 21:15-19). How wonderfully tender of Jesus to restore Peter those three times just as Peter had three times denied ever knowing Jesus. In that act, Peter's broken heart was healed and he was restored to the place that was prepared for him.

Later, we see Jesus sadly questioning another friend, "Judas, are you betraying the Son of Man with a kiss?" (Luke 27:47). Jesus said again to Judas, "Friend, do what you came for" (Matthew 26:50). In that act of a kiss, Judas was making a mockery of their friendship. When you've experienced feelings of betrayal, Jesus can identify and meet you there with healing.

Are you feeling overwhelmed, distressed, in anguish and struggling to surrender to God? Jesus understands because He experienced that, too. "I have a baptism to undergo, and how distressed I am until it is completed" (Luke 12:50). "He began to be deeply distressed and troubled" (Mark 14:33). "My soul is overwhelmed with sorrow to the point of death" (Matthew 26:38). Luke describes Him as "being in anguish" (Luke 22:44). Jesus struggled with surrendering just as we do and finally, after suffering agony to the point of sweating drops of blood, He surrendered it all to His Father. His struggle finally culminated in, "Father, if You are willing, take this cup from me; yet not my will, but Yours be done" (Luke 22:39-45).

Do you struggle with feeling isolated and alone, feeling forsaken by those you desire to understand and be with you? Jesus knows what it feels like, "Then all the disciples deserted Him and fled" (Matthew 26:56). He was abandoned in His greatest time of need. "You will leave me all alone, yet I am not alone for my Father is with me" (John 16:32). The same holds true for us. In our greatest struggle with feeling abandoned and alone, Jesus, the

Father, and the Spirit are with us.

Have you ever experienced having lies told about you and being falsely accused? Jesus understands. "The chief priests and the whole Sanhedrin were looking for false evidence against Jesus so that they could put Him to death" (Matthew 26:59). What did Jesus do when falsely accused? "But Jesus remained silent" (Matthew 26:63). Why? He knew who He was and trusted His Father to ultimately defend Him.

Do you at times feel helpless, weak, and powerless? Jesus knows what it is to feel helpless. "They bound Him and led Him away" (Matthew 27:2). "He was led like a lamb to the slaughter" (Isaiah 53:7). He was crucified in weakness, but He went through it by the power of God so we, too, could have God's strength in our weakness (2 Corinthians 13:4).

Have you struggled with being shamed, mocked, abused, or abandoned? Jesus can identify with the pain, because He was abused. He was stripped, mocked, spit upon, and completely humiliated over and over again (Matthew 27:27-31). Those passing by, the chief priests, elders, teachers, even the thief who was crucified with Him, hurled insults at Him (Matthew 27:39-44). He was beaten beyond recognition (Isaiah 52:14). Worst of all, He cried out, "My God, my God why have you forsaken me?" (Matthew 27:46) Jesus experienced that final abandonment so that we'd have the guarantee of one relationship in which we would never be abandoned. He promises us, "I will never leave you or forsake you" (Hebrews 13:5- end). We are forever accepted!

The Exchange Process

Sometimes the exchange with Jesus is instantaneous, but often it is a process that can take a while as we release the hurts, begin to forgive, and finally replace the lies with His truth. All that Jesus suffered is part of the exchange of the cross (Isaiah 53:43-45). We look to the cross for our salvation and forgiveness from sin, maybe even for our physical healing, but it is also for our emotional healing as well.

"He had no beauty or majesty to attract us to Him, nothing in His appearance that we should desire Him. He was despised and rejected by men, a man of sorrows and familiar with suffering. Like one from whom men hide their faces, He was despised and we esteemed Him not. Surely He took up our infirmities and carried our sorrows, yet we considered Him stricken by God, smitten by Him and afflicted. But He was pierced for our transgressions, He was crushed for our iniquities; the punishment that brought us peace was upon Him, and by His wounds we are healed." (Isaiah 53:1-8)

"The Spirit of the Sovereign Lord is upon me because the Lord has anointed me to preach good news to the poor. He has sent me to bind up the brokenhearted, to proclaim freedom for the captives and release from darkness for the prisoners, to proclaim the year of the Lord's favor and the day of vengeance of our God, to comfort all who mourn and provide for those who grieve in Zion – to bestow a crown of beauty instead of ashes, the oil of gladness instead of mourning and a garment of praise instead of a spirit of despair." (Isaiah 61:1,2)

In Luke 4:16-21, Jesus stood in the synagogue, quoted the above verse, and said, "Today this scripture is fulfilled in your hearing."

What are some of the things we can exchange?

- Our sin for His righteousness (2 Corinthians 5:21)
- Our guilt for His forgiveness and cleansing (1 John 1:9)
- Our broken heart for His mending and restoring (Isaiah 61:1)
- Our feelings of being in imprisoned and in bondage for His freedom (Isaiah 61:1, Galatians 5:1)
- Our feelings of rejection for His acceptance (Isaiah 53:3)
- Our feelings of abandonment and fear of being left all

alone for His belonging (In Matthew 26:56 we see Jesus being left all alone. That is part of what He suffered for us so that John 14:23 could be possible and we could find our home in Him.)

- Our shame identity for a new identity that comes from Him and brings Him glory (Isaiah 54:4 and Colossians 1:27 "Christ IN YOU the hope of glory.")
- Our feelings of loneliness or not fitting in and belonging for the place He prepared for us (In John 16:32 & Luke 9:58, Jesus experienced similar feelings so that John 14:2,3,18 could be possible.)
- Our feelings of feeling overwhelmed for His peace (In Matthew 26:38 Jesus experienced feeling overwhelmed to the point of death so we could experience His peace. John 16:33)
- Our sadness, sorrow and grief for His joy (Isaiah 50:10-11, Isaiah 53:4, Isaiah 61:3)
- Our mourning for His spirit of gladness (Isaiah 61:3)
- Our despair for a garment of praise (Isaiah 61:3)
- Our weakness (powerlessness) for His strength (2 Corinthians 12:9,10 and 13:4)
- Our emptiness for His fullness (Colossians 2:9,10)
- Our feelings of being orphaned for His adoption (John 14:18, 23 Romans 8:15,16)
- Our pain and sickness (spirit, soul, and body) for His healing (Isaiah 53:4,5)
- Our inadequacy for His competency (2 Corinthians 3:5,6)
- Our oppression for His deliverance (Isaiah 53:7,8)
- Our ashes for His beauty (Isaiah 61:3)
- Our false beliefs and lies for His truth (John 16:13)

Replacing the Lies with God's Truth

"I have chosen you, and not rejected you. Fear not, for I am with you; be not dismayed, for I am your God. I will strengthen you, yes, I will help you. I will uphold you with my righteous right hand." (Isaiah 41:9b,10)

"Do not fear, for you will not be ashamed, neither be disgraced for you will not be put to shame. For you will forget the shame of your youth." (Isaiah 54:4)

"Instead of your shame, you shall have double honor. And instead of your confusion, they shall rejoice in their portion. For I, the Lord, love justice; I hate robbery." (Isaiah 61:7,8)

"Even to them, I will give in my house and within my walls a place and a name. Better than sons and daughters, I will give them an everlasting name that shall not be cut off." (Isaiah 56:5) *A name relates to our identity.

"You shall be called by a new name which the mouth of the Lord will bestow. You shall be a crown of glory in the hand of the Lord. You shall no longer be termed forsaken, nor shall your land any more be termed desolate for the Lord delights in you." (Isaiah 62:2,3)

Jesus said, "...I am going there to prepare a place for you." (John 14:2)

"I will not leave you as orphans, I will come to you." (John 14:18)

"If anyone loves me, he will keep my word and my Father will love him and We will come to him and make Our home with him." (John 14:23)

"As the Father loved me, I have also loved you, abide in my love." (John 15:9)

"Oh Lord, you have searched me and known me." (Psalm 139:1)

"For you formed my inward parts, you covered me in my mother's womb. I will praise you, for I am fearfully and wonderfully made. Marvelous are your works. Your eyes saw my substance being yet unformed; and in your book they were written, the days fashioned for me when as yet there were none of them." (Psalm 139:13)

In writing this book, I heard the Lord speaking to us:

"Yes, healing must come to every part of you and go deep within you so that out of your innermost being will come life, real life, My life. If your life is colored by anger, loss, or grief that has not been worked through, not only are you being robbed, but others are as well. Your anger will overflow in illegitimate ways toward yourself and others, causing the robbery of true life.

"See Me as a giver; a giver of life, love, truth, peace, and hope in the midst of your present reality. Hope in Me, in my goodness of heart toward you. Come to Me, trust Me in the pain and allow My river of life to begin to flow first within you to bring healing, and then let it be released out from you even this day. Life, light, truth, love, kindness, and forgiveness, that is My flow. Allow the grief of yesterday to work its work, then wash your face and go on.

"Come to Me today. We will have an adventure even in your own house. Look to Me, be in Me, lose yourself in Me for I am your life, your joy, and the glory that then reflects back to Me."

Prayer for Freedom

Father, thank You for providing in every way for my freedom. Please give me a willing heart and spirit to allow You to do all You desire to bring forth Your life within me. You sent Jesus who paid for the exchange You wish to make with me, but I need the Helper, the Holy Spirit to help me do what I, by myself, cannot. Help me to release my broken heart and allow You to bind me up. Help me to receive Your spirit of adoption in exchange for my pain and forgive all who have hurt me. Help me to remain faithful to You in the process, no matter how long it takes. Introduce me to myself, the one the enemy tried to destroy, and bring me forth into being who You have always known me to be. I desire all this to be done so that my life will bring You much glory. All this is only possible because of Jesus' great sacrifice for me. Thank You, Jesus!

10
FINDING OUR TRUE IDENTITY

Purpose and Destiny

---

*"I will instruct you in the way you should go, I will
counsel you and watch over you." Psalm 32:8
"Teach me to do your will, for you are my God; may your
good Spirit lead me on level ground." (Psalm 143:10)
"I cry out to God Most High who fulfills
His purpose for me..." Psalm 57:2
"When my spirit grows faint within me, it is You who
knows my way." Psalm 142:3*

Due to the twisted ways of the enemy, most of us have tried to find our identity from what we *do* instead of who we *are*. In the beginning, before the fall of man, it was not so. Genesis, the book of beginnings, reveals, "The Lord God formed the man from the *dust* of the ground and *breathed into his nostrils the breath of life*, and man became a *living being*" (Genesis 2:7). Before man ever *did* anything, he simply *was*, having an identity bestowed on him through the breath of God. Then God took the man and put him in the Garden to tend it (Genesis 2:15). Notice that man's *doing* came after his *being*, for it was out of his *being* that God gave Adam his work to *do*. It was work that came from the way he was created and that was uniquely fit for him. "For we are God's workmanship, created in Christ Jesus to do good works, which God prepared in advance for us to do" (Ephesians 2:10).

In my early adulthood, I was pushed by well meaning adults into work that didn't fit me at all and I was miserable! Only after walking with Jesus for a while did I begin to discover my gifts and allow them to make a way for me (Proverbs 18:16 NKJV). As those gifts finally began to rise to the surface in the right atmosphere, others recognized them and validated what I was then enjoying. Man was originally given work that did not include toiling, but instead he lovingly tended the Garden. The toiling (Ecclesiastes 3:1-8) we so often experience came in after Adam and Eve fell (Genesis 3:17-19). How often have you felt stressed in doing a job you love? Even our gifts, when not mingled with His life within us, can become toil. However, as we begin to draw our life from His life, we can once again be Garden tenders, not toilers.

When the fall of man happened (Genesis 3:1-19), the life-giving breath of God that gave true identity to our first parents was lost even though their human breath remained. As a result, life could no longer be drawn from the peaceful breath of God's life within them, but instead it came from the tree of the knowledge of good and evil. That tree had no real life in it at all, only the illusion and appearance of life and the beautiful Garden Adam had lovingly tended was lost to them. Their lives were changed from resting in the provision of God to performing, struggling, toiling, and striving for identity.

Sadly, their choice affected us as well. The way back to God's original intent begins by receiving the breath of God within us, first and foremost through Jesus' awesome sacrifice on the cross, but then we must choose to give up our dependence on even the *good* side of the tree of the *knowledge of good and evil*. Instead, we must begin to draw our life and identity from the only true tree (the tree of Life), which is Jesus, who has been invited to live within us. As Christians, we've received the first part, but too many times we've never given up the tree of the knowledge of good and evil. With the realization of what that "good" tree has produced in our lives and becoming aware of our poverty of spirit, we are ready to turn to Jesus for a new way to live. We can then begin to *draw our life* from Jesus instead of just *doing life* by performing and "being good." We can begin to experience life as it was meant to be lived and return to living as *human beings* instead of *human doings*. "With joy you will draw water (life) from the well of salvation" (Isaiah 12:3 Italics mine).

The first tree, the tree of the knowledge of good and evil, connects to our desire for control, self-protection, and pride through our independence, producing in us a striving and dead religion. The second, the tree of Life, is based on our desperate dependency upon Jesus living in and through us in the unique way He has designed us. From the first tree, we do works *for* God and from the second, God does His works *in* and *through* us. From the first tree, we get the glory for what we've achieved and, from the second, our very lives and works bring glory to Him! Our lives are then lived unto Him and no longer just for our own pleasure. "Thou art worthy, O Lord, to receive glory and honor and power; for Thou has created all things, and for Thy pleasure they are and were created" (Revelations 4:11KJV). As we allow Jesus to set us free, we will be called "oaks of righteousness a planting of the Lord for the display of His splendor" (Isaiah 61:3- end).

As my eyes began to be opened to see this, it made all the difference in my life. Instead of looking somewhere "out there" for life, I began to find my life from the inside out as I recognized Jesus within me and began to discover with wonder the unique way He had designed me. As I finally cooperated with the Spirit in beginning to understand the things that brought me life, I began to see how He created me and desired to join with the Spirit of Truth to fight for the reality of that life. I wasted many years looking for approval and acceptance from "out there" instead of realizing that Christ in me already approves. Because my innermost being is where Life Himself dwells, it's not surprising that the Scriptures reveal that it's from my innermost being that rivers of living water will flow (John 7:38). We are reminded that, "...the kingdom of God is within you" (Luke 17:21).

God has never given up on us no matter how much we've

messed up or given up on ourselves. Instead, He is compelled by His great love for every one of us and His desire to redeem every part of us. He stands patiently waiting, knocking on the door of our hearts (Revelation 3:20), passionately desiring to restore each of us to the original intent for our lives. Thankfully, God sent Jesus to die in order that the way could be opened and received by anyone who desires true life, which is far more than heaven, as wonderful as that will be. "I am... the life," Jesus tells us (John 14:6). Far too often we receive salvation, but seldom allow Him to restore our souls from the wounds of the past so we can more fully participate with Him in fulfilling the Kingdom purposes originally intentioned for our lives.

On the journey of our lives, even as Christians, we can begin to settle for the *good* life that comes from the wrong tree. Jesus made a way for the life-giving breath of God's Spirit to return us to our true identity, even though we might have lost our way without realizing it. John writes about one of Jesus' first acts with His disciples after rising from the dead. He said, "Peace be with you! As the Father has sent me, I am sending you. And with that He breathed on them and said, 'Receive the Holy Spirit'" (John 20:21,22). How wonderful! The breath of God was finally returned to those who received Him (Ezekiel 37:5). Later, we see the Spirit released even more fully, giving us the power *to be* His witnesses (Acts 1:8). Through our partaking of His life (breath) and choosing to live our daily lives by drawing from the life of Jesus within us, we once again can become human *beings* instead of just human *doings*. It is vital we understand this or we will continue to draw our life from the tree of the knowledge of good and evil.

The enemy has deceived us into priding ourselves that we are eating from the good side instead of the evil side of the tree, but sadly it's the wrong tree altogether! The scripture is clear; there is only one who is *good* and that is God alone (Matthew 19:17). It's only when we draw our life from Jesus, the tree of Life Himself, that we are living the life that is truly life!

"For in Him we live and move and have our being" (Acts

17:28). True life is meant to be lived from Him, through Him and unto Him. "I have been crucified with Christ and I no longer live, but Christ lives in me. The life I live in the body, I live by faith in the Son of God, who loved me and gave Himself for me." (Galatians 2:20) "With you (God) is the fountain of life; in your light we see light" (Psalm 36:9).

The Bible reveals what it calls a mystery, which is "Christ in you, the hope of glory" (Colossians 1:27). When we really lay hold of this, Jesus can begin to reflect His life through us in our own unique way and particular gifts. If we will allow Him, Jesus is able to redeem a history of painful circumstances. I lived as a victim for far too many years until finally being willing to enter my pain with Him so I could release it and begin the process of really becoming "me" – the "me" He always knew was there. In choosing to be a victim though, I got pity and an identity of sorts even though it brought me, as well as others, death instead of life. "I have set before you life and death, blessings and curses. Now choose life, so that you and your children might live." (Deuteronomy 30:19) When we are willing to give the pain to Him as an exchange, and as our co-laboring with Jesus begins to happen, our very being brings Him glory. Just as the moon reflects the light of the sun since it has no light in itself, so we will begin more and more to reflect the glory of the Sun of Righteousness who has healing in His wings (Malachi 4:2).

Psalm 4:1 is interesting, "How long, O men, will you turn my glory into shame? How long will you love delusions and seek false gods?" When we receive forgiveness for our legitimate shame and release the lies of our illegitimate or false shame, God is able to replace the shame we have carried with the light of His glory. Our lives are meant to be about Him to bring Him glory, not about us proving ourselves as competent and acceptable by our own striving and performing. "For He chose us in Him before the creation of the world to be holy and blameless in His sight. In love He predestined us to be adopted as His sons through Jesus Christ, in accordance with His pleasure and will-- to the praise of

His glorious grace, which He has freely given us in the One He loves." (Ephesians 1:4) There's more: "in order that we who were the first to hope in Christ might be for the praise of His glory" (Ephesians 1:12). "Not that we are competent in ourselves, but our competence comes from God" (2 Corinthians 3:5). "But we have this treasure in jars of clay to show that this all-surpassing power is from God and not from us" (2 Corinthians 4:7).

Purpose and Destiny

As we begin with more consistency to draw our being from the life of Jesus within us, He can begin to plant us in the garden He has prepared for us to tend. We so often feel that God is far off, but He's closer than our own breath, living through us from within as we allow Him! "The kingdom of God does not come with your careful observation, nor will people say, 'Here it is', or 'There it is,' because the kingdom of God is within you." (Luke 17:20,21) I find that much of the Body of Christ does not deeply grasp the truth of His life within and is still looking for Him afar off. When we lay hold of the truth of His life within, it is truly life changing.

"For we are God's workmanship, created in Christ Jesus to do good works, which God prepared in advance for us to do" (Ephesians 2:10). He alone knows the purposes that each of us was created to fulfill, but our doing must come out of first finding our being in Him. Our purposes are unique to us and can be in any field. They can be bought forth in the home and family, the workplace, the marketplace, the gym, the neighborhood, the coffee shop or anywhere God plants us.

Even though I hate exercise and do it only in order to faithfully care for the body God has given me, I've had a number of divine encounters while working out. Divine encounters are the times you can see the hand of God working in the people He brings to us to talk with. It hasn't been unusual to see someone in tears on the next machine as they pour their heart out. One woman God sent to me at the gym began crying and sharing her story immediately after we met. She had said only, "Hi, my name is...," and a few other sentences before the dam burst. She had been abused and God had been preparing her for our encounter even though neither of us knew it beforehand.

"For I know the plans I have for you, declares the Lord, plans to prosper you and not to harm you, plans to give you hope and a future" (Jeremiah 29:11). For years I quoted verses like that, but didn't understand the lengthy process it would take to make me into the ministry He desired to do in and through me. We don't do ministry, we are the ministry. The man or woman becomes the message. I remember reading somewhere that a speaker was asked how long it took him to prepare his message. His answer was, "My whole life." I can see now how my whole life prepared me for the particular piece I have to bring to the Body of Christ. The part I have to bring actually originated in the pain, loneliness, and hurt of my childhood.

As I was finally willing to allow God to open up my pain so my broken heart could be healed, the transformed pain within me became the ministry God would to bring release to other wounded people as well. "The Lord is close to the brokenhearted, and saves those who are crushed in spirit" (Psalm 34:18). The joy though, is that God uses us for others even while we are still in the process of being healed and restored ourselves.

The Bible reveals the preparation process. "'Just as I watched over them to uproot and tear down, and to overthrow, destroy and bring disaster, so I will watch over them to build and to plant,' declares the Lord" (Jeremiah 31:28). What is it that must be uprooted, torn down, overthrown, and destroyed? Only the creator God who has always known us is wise and skillful enough to cut away that which has been quietly deceiving and destroying us by the "way that seems right to a man" yet leads to death, without destroying our true hearts (Proverbs 14:12). He never destroys the real us, but only the systems we've built to find our worth even though they often feel like us since we've lived with them for so long. He destroys the things in which we've hidden ourselves and those things or people we've used to find our false security and identity. Without the systems ruling us, God is able to begin to rebuild our lives on the strong, firm, secure foundation of Jesus' life within us.

With our survival systems torn down, our true identity is able to come more out of the life of Jesus within us (Colossians 1:27) and His acceptance and love, instead of the old shame-based identity that had to prove itself in order to have worth. We begin to have significance, not out of what we *do*, but because of who we *are*, which is His valuable creation. We begin to recognize that we are known as we truly are with full acceptance and love and that we have always been seen, valued, and fought for from before we were ever born.

Jesus has been standing at the door of our lives, knocking, waiting for us to join Him so as to redeem the past from the hands of the destroyer (1 John 3:8). Then, out of the wonderfully unique way we are created, we can each begin to walk in the purposes ordained for us from before the foundation of the world (Ephesians 1:1-10 & 2:8-10). We can become who we have always been meant to be and fulfill the "days ordained for us" according to His original blueprint. "O Lord, You have searched me and You know me" (Psalm 139:1). "For You created my inmost being; You knit me together in my mother's womb. I praise You because I am fearfully and wonderfully made, I know that full well. My frame was not hidden from You when I was made in the secret place. When I was woven together ... Your eyes saw my unformed body. All the days ordained for me were written in Your book before one of them came to be." (Psalm 139:13-16) Those are the days the enemy tried to steal, kill, and destroy, but are meant to be redeemed because of Jesus the Redeemer who paid the price for us (John 10:10).

As we lay hold of this, our lives and desires begin to reflect more and more the life and desires of Jesus within us, but always through our own wonderful uniqueness and particular gifts. The pain from the past begins to be healed, redeemed, and released through us as broken bread that feeds those He brings to us who are hungry. We are not then giving to others through our great knowledge, but through the redeemed pain and brokenness that brings forth His healing truth and revelation. He is able to increasingly trust us to handle His glory without our falsely using it to prove ourselves worthy. Because we are already worthy in Him, we simply reflect the glory back to Him. A way begins to open within us that allows Him to trust us with the garden He has already prepared for us to tend. We begin to work *with* Him, no longer just *for* Him, to bring forth the piece He has given to us. Our lives become about co-laboring for the coming of His kingdom on the earth as it is in heaven and we do that wherever He happens to plant us.

"Remain in Me, and I will remain in you. No branch can bear fruit by itself, it must remain in the Vine. Neither can you bear fruit unless you remain in Me. I am the Vine you are the branches. If a man remains in Me and I in him, he will bear much fruit; apart from Me you can do nothing." (John 15:4,5)

Destiny: A Journey

"We have the idea that God is going to do some exceptional thing, that He is preparing and fitting us for some extraordinary thing by and by, but as we go on in grace, we find that God is glorifying Himself here and now, in the present minute."
- Oswald Chambers, My Utmost for His Highest.

Destiny is sometimes viewed as a destination or a particular place at which we must arrive. I believe that our destination will one day be attained when we finally arrive home and see Him face-to-face in all His glory. My longing is to hear, "Well done, my good and faithful servant!" In the meantime, as we listen carefully to His voice, submit our hearts to know Him, and walk with Him in the simple way He is calling us, we begin to be transformed from glory to glory. That daily intimate walk with Jesus very simply and quietly begins to fulfill the purposes for which we were created, enabling us to enter into His joy more and more as we cooperate with Him in the larger story He is writing in the earth. We begin to understand how the smaller, sometimes painful story of our lives, as it's being healed and restored, fits uniquely into the wonderful story of redemption that He has purposed from the beginning of time.

Our lives have meaning and purpose that goes far beyond just settling, surviving or creating our own security and significance. All true security and significance is from Him and our lives are meant to flow out from that place to the world around us. We are not just an insignificant dot on the earth. The redemption and uniqueness of each of our lives, joining with His life, is part of something larger than we can imagine. Working with God's Spirit in restoring our souls can enable us to walk out of the curses of past generations into the blessings for future generations, spanning into eternity. Grasping this helps us to join with Him by allowing our lives to be lived daily for His purposes, bringing forth the fruit that remains for eternity. "But you are a chosen generation, a royal priesthood, a holy nation, His own special people that you may proclaim the praises of Him who called you out of darkness into His marvelous light" (1 Peter 2:9).

"Taste and see that the Lord is good; blessed is the man who takes refuge in Him." (Psalm 34:8)

As I wrote this last chapter, I heard God speak to each of us:

"Walk with Me. My desire is for you to walk with Me daily in the cool of My garden. It is really simple because you don't have to know where you are going. You have only to know Me, to trust Me, to remain in Me, and to allow Me to lead you. Let your heart give up its survival systems of self-protection and self-absorption because your real life is not about you, but instead about allowing Me to fulfill My purposes in and through you. All this can happen in the everyday things of life just as you are very simply walking

with Me. My desire is for you to give up hugging the shore and flow with Me today, tomorrow, and into your future. I am the way. Allow the gifts I have put within you to come out in the simplest of ways. Do not be sidetracked by looking for the big opportunity, but just move with Me today. I long for you just as I did for Adam. Come, and we will walk together in the cool of the garden I have prepared for you to tend."

Will we respond to His invitation with, "Yes, Lord, I'll come"?

References

Allender, Dan. *The Wounded Heart*, (Colorado Springs, CO: Navpress, 1990)

Breathitt, Barbie L. *Dream Encounters,* (North Richland Hills, TX: Barbie Breathitt Enterprises, LLC, 2009)

Chambers, Oswald. *My Utmost for His Highest*, (Uhrichsville, OH: Barbour Publishing, Inc., 1935, 1963)

Crabb, Larry. *Shattered Dreams*, (Colorado Springs, CO: Waterbrook Press, 2001)

Curtis, Brent & John Eldredge. *The Sacred Romance*, (Nashville, TN: Thomas Nelson, 1997)

Eldredge, John. *The Journey of Desire,* (Nashville, TN: Thomas Nelson, Nashville)

Eldredge, John. *Waking the Dead,* (Nashville, TN: Thomas Nelson, 2003)

Eldredge, John. *Wild at Heart*, (Nashville, TN: Thomas Nelson, 2001)

Maisenbacher, Rebecca. *If I'm Healed By His Stripes, Then Why Do I Still Hurt?*, (Lakeland, FL: Covenant Publishing House, 2009)

McGee, Robert S. *The Search for Significance*, (Houston, TX: Rapha Publishing, 1990)

Founded in 2009, Covenant Publishing House facilitates publishing projects for writers, artists, musicians and teachers associated with The Covenant Center in Lakeland, Florida (www.thecovenantcenter.com).

The Covenant Center was birthed from a vision given to Richard and Rebecca Maisenbacher that encompasses individuals and groups from various Christian denominations. We believe that the entire Body of Christ is commissioned to go into the world and make disciples.

The ministry vision is to see the Body of Christ strengthened, equipped and restored through emotional, physical and spiritual healing; and to be an expression of worship through the Creative Arts. The Covenant Center's hope is to encourage and train Saints to minister in their gifts and callings - in the community, marketplace, country and throughout the world, sharing the love of Christ.

For further information, and to find other projects of Covenant Publishing House, please contact:

Covenant Publishing House
26 Lake Wire Drive
PO Box 524
Lakeland, Fl. 33802-0524
www.covenantpublishinghouse.com